Institutional Abuse
of
Children & Youth

The *Child & Youth Services* series:

- *Institutional Abuse of Children & Youth,* edited by Ranae Hanson
- *Youth Participation & Experiential Education,* edited by Daniel Conrad and Diane Hedin
- *Legal Reforms Affecting Child & Youth Services,* edited by Gary B. Melton
- *Images of Youth in Literature,* edited by Ruth Stein

Institutional Abuse
of
Children & Youth

Ranae Hanson, Editor

Child & Youth Services
Volume 4, Numbers 1/2

The Haworth Press
New York

The Haworth Press, Inc., 28 East 22 Street, New York, NY 10010

Library of Congress Cataloging in Publication Data
Main entry under title:

Institutional abuse of children & youth.

    (Child & youth services ; v. 4, no. 1/2)
    Includes bibliographical references and index.
    1. Child abuse--United States--Addresses, essays, lectures--Collected works.
2. Children--Institutional care--United States--Addresses, essays, lectures--Collected works. 3. Child abuse--United States--Prevention--Addresses, essays, lectures--Collected works. 4. Children--Civil rights--United States--Addresses,essays, lectures--Collected works. I. Hanson, Ranae. II. Title: Institutional abuse of children and youth. III. Series.
HV701.C47 vol. 4, no. 1/2   [HV741] 362.7s   81-7194
ISBN 0-917724-97-6   [362.7'32'0973]   AACR2

Institutional Abuse
of
Children & Youth

Child & Youth Services
Volume 4, Numbers 1/2

Institutional Abuse
of
Children & Youth

FOREWORD

In this, Volume 4 of *Child & Youth Services*, the journal embarks on a new course. The format, the content, and the focus of the journal have all changed substantially. Previous issues featured a literature review covering one area of the field, followed by abstracts from a wide range of the journal literature relevant to child and youth services. In this issue and in the future, we will provide treatment in depth of a particular subarea of interest in the field, one area per issue.

We still believe in the importance of journal abstracts, particularly in this field where significant contributions are scattered so widely that few, if any, of us can maintain continuing direct access to all of the periodicals where relevant material might appear. We are currently exploring ways in which such a service might be provided on a more systematic, exhaustive basis in the future. As for the literature reviews, we feel that the new format will provide even deeper coverage of areas of emerging interest and concern.

In essence, we will be providing primarily original, "collected readings" presentations in new areas or in those that represent new "slants" or new conceptualizations in the field. This will permit the relatively rapid publication of material on topics that seem underrepresented in the established literature. The current issue, devoted to institutional abuse, is a good example. Forthcoming issues will cover youth participation, child and youth services and the law, and the representation of child and youthwork in literature. The journal is designed to provide text material for use in relevant courses where such a resource is not otherwise readily available, to update those already working in the areas covered, and to illuminate new perspectives for colleagues throughout the field of child and youth services.

With this issue, we also introduce Ranae Hanson as *CYS* Editor. She combines an extensive background in editing and writing with experience in youthwork, most recently as Editor of *The Link: A Newsletter for Youth Service Professionals*, published by The Enablers, a Minnesota coordinating organization serving youth programs and youthworkers. She is cur-

1

rently a research specialist at the Center for Youth Development and Research, University of Minnesota. For each issue, she will work closely with an issue editor, a leader in the particular sphere with which that issue is concerned. For this first issue, she is serving as issue editor as well.

We are always interested in receiving new ideas for topics and nominations (including self-nominations) for issue editors, so your suggestions are invited. Other suggestions, reactions to the journal, and the like are helpful to us and are always welcome, so we look forward to hearing from you. We hope you will find the "New *CYS*" as stimulating, informative, and helpful as its preparation has been for us!

Jerome Beker
Editor-in-Chief

INTRODUCTION

Institutional abuse of children and youth is variously defined: in the narrow sense, as abuse occurring in residential group care settings; in the broad sense, as flowing accidentally from or as an intrinsic element in the operation of our governmental and other social institutions affecting young people; and in other ways, between these extremes. Since definitions have not yet crystallized in this sphere, the papers to follow reflect a variety of definitions and perspectives. What will be evident to the reader, we hope, is the exent to which many of the significant issues transcend the surface distinctions. The residential group care setting, long recognized as a microcosm of life, provides clear examples of abuse that can be related to abuse that occurs elsewhere in society, since both result from similar factors and emerge through the same dynamics.

These issues have only recently emerged into the arena of public scrutiny and become the focus of systematic attention in governmental, professional, and lay circles. The concern appears to have arisen from three major sources: (1) a broadening of interest, previously focused mainly on the family, in child abuse generally; (2) a growing sense that institutions designed to be helpful to abused children and other young people with problems may themselves be abusing; and (3) the influence of various advocacy groups, including those concerned for the needs of minorities and the poor and those concerned with children's rights, which have now begun to focus on institutional issues. These influences are reflected in the priority attention that has been given to this problem by government through the National Center for Child Abuse and Neglect and the National Institute for Juvenile Justice and Delinquency Prevention, and by other groups.

The field is so new that most of those working in it have only begun to clarify their thinking, usually with an overlay from previous experience with family abuse or institutional work—rarely both. They have recently begun to talk to each other, but a professional culture with common definition and understandings has not yet emerged, nor have issues and boundaries been clarified. As a result, the articles that follow represent not only a range of views, but also a range of definitions and levels of analysis. They do not exhaust the topics that might have been encompassed, but we hope that they do provide the reader with an orientation to the people working and interested in this area of concern and to the ideas and perspectives that have begun to emerge as central. In this way, we hope that they can provide the basis for those concerned to begin to move toward the more sophisticated, common understandings needed if the field is to move ahead effectively and to influence for good the way we treat our young people.

The first three articles begin to define the field, the first by categorizing institutional abuse, the second by comparing it with family abuse, and the third by recognizing abuse as any failure to provide for and safeguard the rights of institutionalized children. The next section addresses a specific abuse-related topic, corporal punishment. The articles approach the issue from two perspectives: the analysis of newspaper reports of its use in the schools, and the analysis of current attempts to justify corporal punishment in child care centers on religious grounds.

The third section looks at abuse as it appears in residential treatment. One article considers the health needs of young people in corrections facilities with the view that the non-treatment constitutes neglect. Two articles concern the controversy over psychiatric care of juveniles, one suggesting that hospital psychiatric care is by nature abusive to young people who are status offenders but who are not psychotic. The other argues that to insist on young people's agreement to psychiatric treatment before they are admitted for care is a denial of their right to treatment. The final article in this section proposes that abuse would occur less frequently if institutions would recognize that some young people are not amenable to treatment and establish special living situations for them so they would not frustrate treatment programs.

The fourth section suggests various responses to institutional abuse: reporting, researching, and preventing. One article discusses the process of reporting an incident, another reports on a study of the factors that cause child care workers to abuse children, and the other proposes addressing abuse by setting up standards to prevent its occurrence. Finally, the fifth section contains articles that point to the ways that abuse prevention can itself become abusive. These articles demonstrate how the institutions that respond to abuse in the family can be more abusive of the children than their families were. In addition, the articles should lead readers to the sobering realization that responses to institutional abuse may result in further abuse, just as responses to family abuse sometimes have.

Clearly, the topic is not exhausted by this discussion. We have entered into consideration of the dangers faced by children in care, and we end by realizing that our intrusion, though absolutely necessary, is not without risk. Therefore, these issues demand careful, conscientious attention, lest we lose sight of the welfare of the young people for whose benefit child and youth service institutions have presumably been created.

Jerome Beker and Ranae Hanson

INSTITUTIONAL ABUSE OF CHILDREN IN OUT-OF-HOME CARE

Eliana Gil

ABSTRACT. The author points out that most children in out-of-home care are there because of their parents' problems, not their own, and that even in care those children are not assured safety. She argues that children in care are subjected to physical and sexual abuse, abuse by programming, and abuse by the system in general. One handicap, she says, is that reports about abuse of children in care are not collected, investigated, and studied, and until this is done the problems cannot be addressed.

In the last decade child abuse professionals have been primarily concerned about parental abuse and neglect of children in the family. Occasionally they have referred to foster parents as perpetrators of abuse, but for the most part they ignore the larger issue of institutional attitudes, policies, and situations that infringe on the basic rights of children in out-of-home care or create dangerous situations for those children.

Nationally, there are approximately 500,000 children in care (Horejsi, 1979), most of them because of their parents' inability or unwillingness to provide a safe and nurturing environment for them. Only a small percentage are in care due to their own behavior or disability. Many parents' caretaking roles are hindered by illness, psychiatric disturbances, or drug and alcohol dependencies, and a significant number of childeren are phys-

Eliana Gil is Assistant Project Director at the San Francisco Child Abuse Council, Inc., 4093 24th Street, San Francisco, CA 94114. Requests for reprints should be addressed to Eliana Gil at that address.

ically or sexually abused or neglected. In California, 46% of the 27,000 children in care are there due to abuse or neglect, for example (1978). Other children simply have no available relatives and must enter a system where the institution serves as parent.

While the intent of the social welfare and juvenile justice systems is to protect and care for these children, they have not fulfilled their promise. The assumption that a child is removed from an abusive or neglectful home and placed in a safe environment can no longer be taken at face value; the fact is that children are often physically abused, neglected, exploited, sexually misused, and disregarded in placement by caretakers appointed to provide a positive rehabilitative experience for them.

Institutional Child Abuse Reporting

There are no hard data to indicate the extent of abuse and neglect of children in out-of-home care.[1] However, lack of data does not mean that there is no problem, since the systems for collecting and recording data about institutional abuse have been grossly inadequate and inconsistent. For one thing, although physical abuse, neglect, and sexual abuse are legally reported offenses no matter who is responsible for them, a surprising number of professionals treat abuse by parents in the home more harshly than they treat abuse by caretakers outside the home. In addition, informal arrangements have frequently given social service licensing and placement departments jurisdiction over complaints of child abuse occurring to children in placement. There is conflict of interest when licensing workers investigate those facilities they have licensed and with which they have established a relationship. Further, most licensing workers are not trained in child abuse investigation procedures.

For the past 3 years the San Francisco Abuse Council, a private nonprofit organization, has been addressing this problem in California. When the Council first began the project in a six-county target area, an evaluation unit from the State Department of Social Services reviewed reports of child abuse in institutions from the previous 5 years. Virtually no reports had been documented through the child abuse reporting system, although many "informal" incident reports were included in licensing and place-

---

[1]A soon to be released HHS study on the incidence of child abuse and neglect nationally will provide "best guess estimates" about the true incidence of child abuse and neglect in the U.S. However, in this study, there were several significant exclusions in the data gathering, among them the exclusion of abuse and neglect in institutions (Child Protection Report, Vol. VI, 23, Nov. 21, 1980).

ment files. At this point the Council specifically requested that the six counties cooperate to record institutional abuse cases, and in 2 years 75 cases were reported and documented. Physical abuse or neglect accounted for 77% of the reports, and sexual abuse accounted for the remaining 23%. Clearly, when reports are encouraged and accepted, they come in.

During those 2 years, the Council provided 140 training sessions on child abuse prevention in out-of-home care. Those caretakers and foster parents who attended spoke of the stress that can contribute to abuse incidents. Obviously, if abuse is reported and analyzed, some of these contributing factors may be correctable.[2]

To further aid in the collection of abuse reports, the Child Abuse Council staff clarified the reporting procedures by requesting an addition to the California reporting law specifying that abuse and neglect of children in out-of-home care be reported to the Child Protection Service, to probation officers, or to the police for investigation. Under this law the Department of Justice was assigned to work with the State Department of Social Services to rewrite regulations so that licensing authorities no longer have a dual role of licensing and also investigating child abuse complaints.[3]

The San Francisco Child Abuse Council defines institutional abuse as any system, program policy, procedure, or indvidual interaction with a child in placement that abuses, neglects, or is detrimental to the child's health, safety, or emotional and physical well-being or in any way exploits or violates the child's basic rights. This abuse of children in out-of-home care is of three types: physical and sexual abuse, program abuse, and system abuse.

Physical Abuse

The most obvious category of abuse is the first—physical, sexual, and emotional abuse like that which occurs in the home but which is perpetrated by a professional caretaker or foster parent. Such cases occur with enough frequency to be a concern. When they are investigated, their contributing factors are often clear.

---

[2]These stresses are discussed in a booklet entitled "Prevention of Abuse and Neglect of Children in Out-of-Home Care," available by writing the State Office of Child Abuse Prevention, 744 P Street, Sacramento, CA 95814.

[3]This law took effect January 1, 1981 and has potential for duplication in other states. Information about it and other Council activities can be obtained by writing The San Francisco Child Abuse Council, 4093 24th St., San Francisco, CA 94114.

For example, a foster mother who had helped many children was asked to take an enuretic, emotionally disturbed child into her care. She was neither trained nor prepared to handle a child with special needs; however, other options for this child were virtually nonexistent, so the woman acquiesced to the worker's plea to accept the child. The child wet his bed every night for 4 months; the foster mother consulted a doctor, did not give the child anything to drink prior to his bedtime, spent considerable time with the child to allay his fear—all to no avail. She had to wash the linen every morning; the house began to smell like urine; she got no help from the worker; her frustration rose. The woman had become attached to the child in spite of the difficulty he presented with bedwetting, yet in the middle of the night, after a particularly difficult day and a fight with her husband about the child, she forced the child to drink his urine and hit him hard enough to leave bruises. This was abusive by almost anyone's standards; yet the contributing factors are clear.

First of all, the child should not have been placed in this home, since the foster parent was not prepared to deal with a special needs child. Secondly, the worker underrated the difficulty of caring for the child in order to place the child. After that, the worker did not assist in problem solving, so the foster parents felt isolated and frustrated. In addition, the woman's relationship with her husband was strained because of the child. Finally, when questioned, the woman related having witnessed her own parents using the same technique to toilet train her brother.

Such abuse does not happen without cause. In addition to protecting children, reporting and investigating cases helps to isolate contributing factors so they can be addressed.

Program Abuse

The second type of abuse and neglect of children in out-of-home care occurs when programs within a facility are below normally accepted standards; have extreme or unfair policies; or rely on harsh, inhumane, or unusual techniques to teach or guide children.

Children going into placement will inevitably experience the trauma of separation and fear of abandonment, which will affect their self-esteem and confidence (Litner, 1976). They may display extremes of certain behavior, such as violence or apathy. If staff do not have basic information about the behavior of children in care and do not know appropriate responses, they cannot provide quality care to children or prevent child maltreatment.

In one case, a 14-year-old boy in an institution had the habit of masturbating. Because the staff could not tolerate the boy's sexual activity, they gave him large doses of Haldol. Records of administration of drugs were loosely maintained in this institution, and no written policy about issuing medications was available, so when staff people were unaware of how much medication had already been given, they simply gave him more. The child received so much medication that his body reacted in a way that looked like a psychotic episode. The staff diagnosed his behavior as "severe psychotic episode," and the boy was moved to a facility designed for psychotic patients, which the boy was not.

In 1979 testimony offered at the Senate Subcommittee of Child and Human Development hearings in California cited overmedication of children as a primary concern, along with inappropriate isolation, mechanical restraint, and disciplinary techniques. Without written standards for the use of medication, isolation, restraint, and discipline, as well as for the general operation of facilities, abuse is likely to occur. There should also be mechanisms for monitoring adherence to standards.

In addition, staff need and desire ongoing training so they can deal with the difficult behaviors exhibited by children in placement. Children who come into care may have had difficult lives that make them fear to trust and establish close relationships. Staff must be trained to deal with this.

System Abuse

Perhaps the most difficult type of abuse to define, acknowledge, or correct is that perpetrated not by any single person or program, but by the immense and complicated child care system, stretched beyond its limits and incapable of guaranteeing safety to all children in care. These child welfare and juvenile justice systems, which remove, place, and decide on the future of children and families, are fraught with shortcomings.

The greatest problem is that children in care tend to remain in care. Two recent publications, *Who Knows? Who Cares? Forgotten Children in Foster Care: A Report of the National Commission on Children in Need of Parents* (1979) and *Children without Homes: An Examination of Public Responsibility to Children in Out-of-Home Care*, confirm the irresponsible management of children in care. This produces "foster care drift"; children tend to stay in care. The average number of placements for a child is five. Due to ill-defined and passive efforts at family reunification or permanency planning, many children remain in care until maturity.

In California, a youth named Dennis Smith sued the Alameda County

Department of Social Services and school district because they failed to find adoptive parents for him (he had been in 16 different placements) and because he had been labelled "educationally handicapped and educationally retarded," although he was not (case reported by the Youth Law Center). This suit sought to place the responsibility for drift on the planners of foster children's lives, and it attempted to point out the immense long-term impact of such neglect. Child advocates search for system reforms and suggest solutions, though these are difficult to implement in the massive and often impersonal child welfare system.

A girl named Sarah provides another example of this problem. At 8 months of age, Sarah was taken to a hospital for a fractured arm, three fractured ribs, and numerous bruises and cigarette burns. She was hospitalized for 10 days and then put in a foster home. Then, after she had experienced two foster home changes and her 20-year-old mother had had considerable counseling, she was replaced in her biologic home at the age of 18 months. Within 5 months, abuse was diagnosed again. After a short hospital stay, she was placed in a fourth foster home. Between 23 months and 55 months of age, she had three subsequent foster home changes. The mother was not willing to voluntarily give up her daughter, and the mother's willingness to use prescribed intervention seemed to make the case for termination of her parental rights untenable. Finally, when Sarah was 55 months old, her mother relinquished parental rights, and adoption plans were begun. An evaluation of Sarah at this time revealed a child, probably of normal intelligence, who was functioning about 1 year behind her chronological age. An attractive little girl, she displayed indiscriminately quick affectionate behavior towards friends and strangers. Psychiatric evaluation revealed a seriously disturbed child, prepsychotic, who had minimal capacity for object relations, and who had demonstrated repeated acting out behaviors in foster care, which resulted in the repeated failures of foster home placement.

This story of Sarah is not surprising to any CPS worker. The abuse and neglect to which she was subjected in infancy were harmful, but how much more harmful were her experiences once she entered the helping system? In less than 5 years, she had experienced eight changes in homes. She had had to adapt to nine mother figures; she had never lived more than 19 months with any single one of them. When Sarah was in foster care, none of the surrogate mothers could, or would, become a psychological mother to her, for their role was a temporary one. Though she was safe from physical assault, she never really had the investment and commitment which is normal with biologic parents. At 55 months of age, she was clearly not a good candidate for adoption.

All three types of abuse—physical, program, and system abuse—must be addressed. The major need, however, is for the definition of child abuse and neglect to include institutional attitudes, policies, and situations that hurt children, harm family integrity, and infringe on basic rights. Professionals and lay people must reassess their actions and attitudes. As a result of the San Francisco Child Abuse Council's activities, many system personnel have remarked, "I always knew these problems were there, but I never knew what to call them and never quite recognized the impact on children's lives."

REFERENCES

Abuse and neglect of children in institutions, 1979. Hearings Before the Subcommittee on Child and Human Development of the Committee of Labor and Human Resources, U.S. Ninety-Sixth Congress, First session on Examination of the Problems of Abuse and Neglect of Children Residing in Institutions or Group Residential Settings, January 4, 1979. Washington, DC, May 31, 1979.

Child abuse and neglect: California's mandatory reporting law. The Central Reporting Registry, 1978.

Children without homes: An examination of public responsibility to children in out-of-home care. Children's Defense Fund, 1520 New Hampshire Avenue, N.W., Washington, DC 20036.

Horejsi, C. *Foster family care: A handbook for social workers, allied professionals, and concerned citizens.* Illinois: Charles C. Thomas, 1979.

Littner, N. *Some traumatic effects of separation and placement.* Child Welfare League of America, Inc., 1976.

Who knows? Who cares? Forgotten children in foster care. Report of the National Commission on Children in Need of Parents, 801 2nd Avenue, New York, NY 10017.

Youth Law Center, 693 Mission Street, San Francisco, CA. Walker, R. and English, A., Attorneys.

INSTITUTIONAL CHILD ABUSE FROM A FAMILY SYSTEMS PERSPECTIVE: A WORKING PAPER

Roderick Durkin

ABSTRACT. The author points out that the victims and perpetrators of abuse in institutions are in many significant ways similar to the victims and perpetrators of abuse in homes. He indicates that, therefore, systems therapy may be effective in institutions as it is in families and suggests ways this could be done. Finally, he describes the Seattle Day Nursery as one program that tries to alleviate the stresses in both families and agencies that lead to abuse.

In our attempt to address the problems caused by institutional abuse, we can be aided by one important fact: child abuse in institutions shares many of the characteristics of child abuse in the home. Thus, we are not confronting an entirely unknown phenomenon when we turn from easing abuse in the family to easing that in out-of-home care. In addition, there may be ways of attacking both at the same time.

The Victims

Few studies have been done about the characteristics of children who are abused in institutions, but we do know that they are usually older than children who are abused in the home and that they are part of an already select population of children for whom it is difficult to care. Beyond that, they may have characteristics similar to those of children who are abused at home.

It seems clear that not just any child is abused; in many homes, one is singled out and is the object of repeated abuse (Gil, 1970). The victim is often perceived by the parent as different (Helfer, 1973). Victims of family

Roderick Durkin is Director of Research, Seattle Day Nursery Association, 302 Broadway, Seattle, WA 98122. Requests for reprints should be addressed to Roderick Durkin at P.O. Box 57, Jamaica, VT 05343.

abuse tend to be difficult children who may have been irritating or prema-
ture babies or have had medical or dietary problems requiring special
care. In institutions as well as at home, abused children appear not to be
chosen randomly, but to be children who are aggravating to their caregivers (Steele & Pollock, 1968).

This research would imply that happy, healthy, and responsive children
who are easier for parents and child care workers to care for will probably
be less frequently abused than unhappy, sickly, sullen children. From this
perspective, caretakers who promote growth and development in children
and help children to be happy and responsible may be reducing the likelihood that the children will be abused.

For this to occur, adversary relationships between children and adults
need to be downplayed, yet institutional responses to problem children
often promote adversary relationships between children and staff. What
clinicians perceive as "clinical planning," youngsters often regard as
"scheming." If children strongly resist the actions caretakers use to help
control them, such as breaking up children's relationships to protect them
or giving them make-believe jobs to build up their self-esteem, then those
children will more likely become targets for abuse.

An alternative treatment goal that might be both positive and achiev-
able would be to promote competence in children. The techniques for
promoting competence in technical skills and interpersonal relationships
are better known and more agreed upon than are techniques for treating
pathology. Moreover, in competency-based programs children are likely
to be motivated to want to do what they need to do (Fromm, 1944).
Promoting individual competence and dealing with psychopathology only
as it interferes with the pursuit of competence are likely to gain the
cooperation and active involvement of youngsters in their own "treatment." This type of program would bring out the best rather than the
worst in children—and thus in child care workers and in parents.

Abusers: The Other Victims

Too often, institutional work brings out the worst in child care workers.
Treatment programs often take children who are miserable, and who may
have been abused, and help them become more contented, easier to live
with. However, as a child in a residential treatment program pointed out,
it does not do that for treatment staff. The boy said that when child care
staff start work, they are happy and enthusiastic and even enjoy the
70-hour work week. Conversely, the children come in messed up, angry,

depressed, strung out on drugs. After a few years, the children leave feeling better about themselves and life in general, while the child care staff leave drinking heavily, wrecking their cars, getting divorced, flunking out of school, and the like.

Child care work is not an easy job, and it is made more problematic by the conditions under which child care workers are often forced to operate. They are usually overworked and underpaid. On the other hand, clinical staff usually work from 9 to 5, and since the children are in school from 9 to 3, those two groups have little contact. Essentially, then, child care staff run the institutions and work with the children for 16 hours a day and on weekends, a responsibility for which they do not receive commensurate pay. In addition, the medical model and its democratized version, the team approach, let the "other professionals" (those with PhDs and MSWs as well as those with MDs) tell child care workers what to do, often without telling them how to do it or how to handle incompatible directives. In the effort to be therapeutic for individual children, child care workers are often asked to implement a variety of treatment plans that cannot be contained under one roof. The workers are left in an isolated position, where power over children becomes their only possibility of attaining any real sense of significance.

No wonder some of them abuse children! They are in social-psychological positions much like those of abusive parents who, while relatively heterogeneous in ethnicity and economic status, are quite similar in attitudes, childhood experiences, and self-concept. Just as, for example, abusive unwed mothers, often children themselves, are isolated from family and community, lack a support system, and hang on the ragged edge financially and emotionally, so child care workers are isolated, unsupported, underpaid, and overstressed. Abusive parents tend to have low self-esteem (Caulfield, Disbrow, & Smith, 1977); to lack an ability to form trusting relationships (Helfer, 1973; Steele, 1975; Ebling, 1975); to be socially isolated (Caulfield, 1977); to be unable to empathize with the child (Hoffman & Salstein, 1967); to have a sense of righteousness about child discipline (Disbrow, 1969; Ebling & Hill, 1975); and to have a low tolerance for frustration (Ebling & Hill, 1975).

Abuse seems to occur when adults are unable to cope with the stress under which they live and take out their frustrations on troublesome, vulnerable children. Other than decreasing the vulnerability of the children, we can address the problem in two ways: by changing the coping mechanisms of the adults or by relieving the strains that are placed on them. Given our as yet limited success in treating psychological problems, it may be more fruitful to mitigate the stresses the abusers experience rather than to try to change their personalities.

The Systems: In Need of Therapy

Child abuse is, in my opinion, best prevented in the context of the larger social system. An act of abuse is the result of many forces that lead to that specific incident. These forces must be changed by developing more functional social systems. Systems-oriented family therapy does not seek to change an individual's pathology, but to diminish its salience for the family by altering the social system so that it does not exacerbate existing pathology and by creating greater symptom tolerance within the family. This is a less ambitious goal than changing pathology; it is both more feasible and more expedient. The same approach may work for institutions.

Preventing continued abuse of institutionalized children is complex, however, usually requiring major structural changes in the institutions. It may seem easier and more politically expedient to fire individual perpetrators of abuse, but this would not be as fruitful as changing the system. Although such change is far more complicated, it need not require additional funding, and such a reorganization of the social system of children's institutions may, in fact, provide better service more cheaply while lessening the incidence of child abuse. To achieve this, we must address the strains that are placed on child care workers: conflicting demands, too much work, too few rewards.

The conflicting demands may be due to the incompatibility of attempts to *treat* children and *raise* children at the same time in the same setting (Durkin & Durkin, 1975). Thus, our attempt to combine individual therapy with a residential milieu may have been ill-advised. Perhaps such therapy needs to be conducted more privately, with fewer attempts to structure the environment according to therapeutic considerations. Child care work could be allowed to proceed developmentally according to the dictates of individual and group work considerations, without having its activities constrained by the requirements of formal therapy. As we have attempted to integrate them, the effectiveness of both child care and therapy appear to have suffered.

The European *educateur* could offer one model for upgrading the role of child care workers and thus reducing the stress of the child care role. The *educateur* is a trained generalist; an overseer of the group life, who organizes daily routine; a confidante; and an educator in the broadest sense. The *educateur* is the "hub of the wheel" and uses physicians, psychologists, social workers, psychiatrists, and educational specialists on a consultative basis. As the repository of most of the information about the children and the person in closest contact with them, the *educateur* has the responsibility and commensurate training and authority to organize the children's lives.

This system is in marked contrast with the inefficient and stressful pyramid organizations we now use, where clinical staff and others who have the least working knowledge of the children's everyday lives make the most far-reaching decisions about their lives. Several have suggested changes in this ineffective model. Goldenberg (1971) describes how the founders of the Residential Youth Center explicitly chose to avoid the pitfalls inherent in the pyramidal organization by developing a horizontal structure of generalists, each of whom had comprehensive administrative, clinical, and residential responsibilities to the client and the family. Linton (1971) reviews the literature on the *educateur* model and makes a strong case for the use of this concept in American institutions. Rieger and Devries (1974) also argue for the use of a generalist child care worker experienced in child care, education, and clinical development, and they describe the development of a training program for such specialists at Camarillo Children's Treatment Center in California. Finally, Barnes (1973) describes the conceptual clarity, body of knowledge, and skills provided by the *educateur* model and contrasts them with the confusion and ambiguity that exist in the role of child care worker.

If clinical staff were used as these authors suggest, primarily as consultants, the money saved could be used to upgrade the position of child care worker. This would provide the potential for workers to develop a serious career in child care and for attracting appropriately trained and motivated individuals. Such a restructuring would reduce the role strains inherent in the positon now and would improve the quality of care by placing a greater emphasis on providing a normalizing experience and gaining cooperation from the children. The professional child care specialist or *educateur* model would also lessen the powerlessness and isolation that have proven so detrimental to institutional abuse of children.

One Agency's Attempt to Reduce Family and Institutional Abuse

The Seattle Day Nursery Association's care and treatment program tries to relieve the stresses that lead to both family and institutional abuse. It takes in children who have been abused in their families, but it is not a residential program. It attempts to keep the children in their homes and to keep them from being abused further, both when they are at home and when they are at the center. Toward the end, a major goal is to promote the normal growth and development of the children. Happy, healthy, and responsive children are more "acceptable"; it is easier for parents and child care workers to care for them.

A second goal is to relieve the stress experienced by the children's parents. Abusive parents have 8 hours a day, 5 days a week, of respite from their children and have emergency respite care available upon request. The program conspicuously disentangles itself, except where stipulated by law, from the punitive, threatening, and coercive approach of many agencies dealing with abusive families, in order to try to avoid an adversary relationship and to develop the rapport necessary to help, and it advocates for its families with regard to their legal, medical, financial, drug, and welfare problems. It helps them to develop networks of formal and informal support systems. Casework services are also provided. Finally, it helps families to improve their parenting skills, which reduces stress by making parenting easier. This dovetails with the "caring" for the children to make them more "acceptable" children, and analogies to the needs of institutional child care staff can easily be seen.

Though the involved parents are provided with individual, group, or systems-oriented therapy, this treatment is separated from the rest of the program by a barrier of strict confidentiality. Individual therapy is offered on the assumption that the best thing parents can do for children is to lead full, happy lives themselves. Family therapy is offered to change dysfunctional, abusive family interaction. It tends not to be threatening or stigmatizing, and if offers a relatively quick return in improving family life and lessening the risk of further abuse. Therapists have no contact with the family or the child, except in therapy; therapy and the other activities both benefit from this separation.

In addition, children in the program are protected at home by the fact that they are picked up from and returned to the home each day. This ongoing observation is a deterrent to abuse and affords better protection than a system of spot checks by overworked Children's Protective Service workers. The continuous contact with the family helps the program to anticipate crises and to intervene before abuse occurs. Finally, daily behavior ratings and a cursory medical checklist at the beginning and end of each day provide an ongoing record of the child's well-being.

Further, the careful recruitment of child care staff, their vigorous support as highly appreciated professionals, and systematic attempts to reduce their "role strain" all help protect the children from institutional abuse. However, there are severe constraints on what even a well-intentioned agency can do to reduce the role strains experienced by child care workers. The nation's low priority on quality child care is reflected in the general disregard for day care, the reimbursement formulas, and the lack of economically and socially viable careers in child care. Child care workers are expected to drive a $10,000 van with 10 infants and toddlers, go into potentially dangerous neighborhoods and homes, deal with difficult and sometimes dangerous parents, implement developmentally oriented Individual Educational Treatment Plans, monitor and care for sick children or children with medical or nutritional problems, feed children, change dirty diapers, attend meetings, and keep up with the unavoidably large amount of paper work. For this they receive at best a marginally livable wage. One agency, despite its best efforts, can do little to change this and must often exploit the enthusiasm, humanitarian concerns, and good will of its child care staff. These factors contribute to a role strain, with the predictable burnout, high rate of turnover, and greater risk of child abuse.

The Seattle program does all it can to reduce the role strains. The director has had many years of child care work experience and fully appreciates the difficulties. Staff members are chosen for such sensitivity. The child care workers are well trained in promoting normal growth and development and in working with parents, and they are not constrained by being expected to be therapists for parents or children. They receive vigorous support and recognition from the agency, which lessens their need to "milk" the children for the satisfactions that these abused and thus often difficult children frequently cannot give. Finally, child care workers are encouraged to ventilate their strong feelings of rage toward parents who undo their good work and their anger, guilt, despair, and frustration about the children's situations and their own working conditions. All of these efforts are designed not only to prevent further abuse, but also to maximize their positive contributions to growth and development.

The agency does not assume responsibility for providing child care staff with therapy. At times it is difficult to maintain this distinction, as workers' personalities are so intimately involved with their work. For example, what is the difference between helping a worker ventilate pent-up job frustrations and doing therapy? As with parents, however, therapy and work are best separated. On the assumption that it is always easier not to hire than to fire, child care workers are carefully screened for serious personal problems. When problems are encountered after hiring, they are cancelled out with sensitivity, fairness,and firmness.

In summary, care and treatment programs should seek to reduce the stress that leads to child abuse—the isolation, powerlessness, and role strains that those who care for children in the home or in institutions experience. Since child abuse is caused, to a large extent, by the roles that victims and perpetrators of abuse fill in the systems of which they are a part, abuse can be effectively addressed through systems change.

REFERENCES

Barnes, F. *An American application of the European education concept.* Paper presented at the Association of Psychiatric Services for Children, Chicago, November 16, 1973.

Caulfield, C., Disbrow, M. A., Smith, M. Determining indicators of potential for child abuse and neglect: Analytical problems in methodological research. *Communicating Nursing Research*, 1977, *10*, 141-162.

Disbrow, M. A. Deviant behavior and punitive reference persons: Child abuse as a special case. In L. Notter (Ed.), *Fifth nursing research conference reports.* New York: American Nurses' Association, 1969, 246-322.

Durkin, R., & Durkin, A. Evaluating residential treatment programs for disturbed children. In Struening & Guttentag, *The handbook of evaluative research* (EIS). Beverly Hills, CA: Sage Publications, 1975.

Ebling, N., Hill, D. (Eds.). *Child abuse: Intervention treatment.* Acton, MA: Publishing Sciences Group, Inc., 1975.

Fromm, E. Individual and social origins of neurosis. *American Sociological Review*, 1944, *9*, 380-384.

Goldenberg, I. *Build me a mountain: Youth poverty and the creation of new settings.* Cambridge, MA: M.I.T. Press, 1971.

Gil, D. *Violence against children.* Massachusetts: Harvard University Press, 1970.

Helfer, R. The etiology of child abuse. Part II. *Pediatrics*, April 3, 1973, *51*, 4.

Hoffman, M. L., & Saltstein, H. D. Parent discipline and the child's moral development. *Journal of Personality and Social Psychology*, 1967, *5*, 5-57.

Linton, T. The educateur model: A theoretical monograph. *Journal of Special Education*, 1971, *5*(2), 155-190.

Rieger & Devries. The child mental health specialist: A new profession. *American Journal of Orthopsychiatry*, 1974, *44*, 150-158.

Steele, B., & Pollock, C. Psychiatric study of parents who abuse infants and small children. In R. F. Helfer & C. H. Kempe (Eds.), *The Battered Child.* Chicago: University of Chicago Press, 1968, 129.

Steele, B. *Working with abusive parents from a psychiatric point of view.* USDHEW Publ. No. (OHD), 70-75, 1974.

THE RESPONSIBILITY OF RESIDENTIAL PLACEMENTS FOR CHILDREN'S RIGHTS TO DEVELOPMENT

George Thomas

ABSTRACT. The author argues that abuse cannot be defined or corrected until the rights of children in institutions are set down. He says that institutions must be held to higher standards in the provision of care for children than are families and classifies children's rights as protection and sustenance, development, and correction intervention. The writer then enumerates the distinction between evaluations of abuse in institutions and in families. Finally, he sets forth some steps by which he feels the reporting and investigation of child abuse cases can be improved.

Introduction

This paper comprises an attempt to assist states in rethinking their approaches to the protection, care, and development of children in residential placement. This is a working paper—nothing more, nothing less—that represents the author's best effort at sorting through and making sense of a matter that we as a people have made very confusing and complex over the course of time.

I began this work in what seemed a logical enough manner, by compiling pertinent state law, licensing regulations, and agency program policies and procedures covering various state agencies and departments that operate or supervise residential placements for children throughout the eight southeastern states composing DHEW's Region IV, the overall domain of inquiry. I wanted to determine how each state was currently addressing the issue of institutional child abuse and neglect, to draw out what appeared to be promising approaches and practices, and to draft these best practices into a suggested model for addressing the problem.

George Thomas is President of the Regional Institute of Social Welfare Research, 455 North Milledge Avenue, Athens, GA 30603; this article was condensed by Ranae Hanson, editor of *Child and Youth Services*. Requests for reprints should be addressed to George Thomas.

This approach proved impractical because it soon became obvious that best practices were in short supply. Among other things, more than one state's mandated agency had not as yet adopted a discernible policy or approach to dealing with institutional child abuse and neglect. Further, judging by the available materials in print, numerous other state departments involved in residential placements, such as Mental Health, Youth Services, and the like, have as yet scarcely addressed the issue. Finally, most licensing regulations do not deal with the topic directly.

Moreover, it was recognized at this juncture that even if the initial approach had proved useful, the outcome would simply have been codification in more general form of practices already being carried out formally or otherwise in many places. Compilations of this sort frequently have a deadening rather than stimulating effect upon our thinking. Worse yet, the presentation of practices in a seemingly authoritative document has, on occasion, led to the justification of current practices of dubious merit.

Having reached this impasse, the decision was made to start over, at what was thought, at that time, to be the beginning, namely, the drafting of a definition of institutional child abuse and neglect that could serve as a base and guide for formulating recommended approaches and practices. This decision led to Part II of this paper, where criteria are identified for determining child abuse and neglect in residential settings that are distinctly different in emphasis from those used to assess occurrences in the family and community context. Unfortunately, it became apparent that enforceable and effective standards cannot be written unless one first identifies the specific rights of children which these standards are intended to implement. Thus, Part I points out that children's rights to achieve basic development goals are the capstone of all other rights of children while they are in residential placements. Finally, Part III presents a number of feasible steps to improve the reporting and investigation of child abuse and neglect in residential placements.

This paper presents a perspective on the role of the Child Protective Services (CPS) agency which is, by implication, both smaller and more realistic than that thrust upon and expected of that agency in most states today. In recent years public awareness about the problems of child abuse and neglect has grown phenomenally, and public expectations about the role of the CPS agency have grown accordingly. As an ever greater number of adult behaviors are being interpreted as abusive or neglectful, the CPS agency is turned to as the logical instrument for coping with this widening definition of deviant behavior. This places an ever increasing burden upon the CPS agency to stretch its protective umbrella across more and more types and incidents of adult-child interaction, and the agency finds itself in a condition of mounting stress because it is not equipped by statute or policy to meet this demand for expansion.

Thus, in the process of examining children's rights, we are driven back to the realization that the CPS agency is responsible for assuring only certain segments of children's rights, namely, those pertinent to physical protection and sustenance and to protection from unwarranted therapeutic or control interventions while in residential placements. The role of the CPS agency in the larger scheme of things is to assure that the standards it adopts to effect physical protection, sustenance,and protection from unwarranted corrective interventions are such that they contribute to, rather than detract from, the achievement of basic development goals. Thus, the CPS agency should assure not just a safe, but also a stable or permanent, residential placement.

I. *Children's Rights to Development: The Governing Principle for Residential Placements*

Standards for determining whether children are being properly served in residential care must be derived from an understanding of the rights of children in our society. Because children are considered dependent, responsibility for their rights is vested primarily in the family. When children's families demonstrate that they will not or cannot carry out their responsibilities, the state assumes a large role in child rearing. Yet, whether children are in their own homes or in state-executed placements, their rights do not change. However, when the state assumes responsibility for rearing children, it must be held accountable to far stricter standards in providing for the children than are the children's families.

We begin with the single proposition that all children have a common right to access to a developmental pathway to productive adult citizenship, consistent with their individual capacities. This proposition serves as an organizing principle for all possible statements of children's rights. It rivets attention upon the most salient feature of childhood, namely, the developmental progression from utter bio-social dependency to functional independence.

The rearing of children in residential care must assure their progression along the developmental pathways towards adulthood. Conversely, acts that distort children's pathways or impede their progress are abusive or neglectful.

Based on that general proposition, we propose the following as the rights of all children:

1. All children have the right to protection and sustenance, which are preconditions to personal development.

2. All children have the right to achieve basic developmental goals consistent with their individual abilities, goals of individualization, socialization, and cognitive preparation.

3. All children have the right to receive corrective interventions to overcome impediments to developmental progress, that is, they have a right to therapeutic intervention and control.

The first and third rights are supportive of the second, which is the core: all efforts must be directed toward implementing that right to achieve basic developmental goals.

Up to the present, we have as a society busied ourselves with the first and third rights, finding ways to protect children from physical harm and to guarantee them their basic material needs and engaging in exhaustive debate and litigation on such issues as children's right to treatment and the appropriateness of various forms of behavioral control. We have spent far less time and effort on the heart of the matter, which involves defining and assuring the rights of children to achievement of developmental goals related to individualization, socialization, and cognitive preparation. We should not work to protect children from physical harm or neglect as an end in itself, but rather, we should do so in order to enhance prospects that children may be better able to achieve basic developmental goals.

This is not simply an exercise in supplanting an essentially negative (reactive) view of state intervention with a more positive (proactive) view. This difference of perspective makes a material difference in the kinds of standards that are adopted to assure the implementation of children's rights, which will be obvious later in this article.

Children's Rights to Protection and Sustenance

Children have the right to be raised by at least one interested parent or other adult in a consistent and stable relationship within a context free of occurrence or threat of physical harm or environmental hazard. In addition, all children have a right to adequate shelter, clothing, nutrition, and medical and dental care. The fulfillment of these rights to protection and sustenance is a necessary precondition to the achievement to basic developmental goals. Any material failure to assure these rights may jeopardize a child's chances for achievement.

However, fulfilling these rights will not guarantee a child's achievement. This point would be of little importance were it not for the fact that governments at all levels currently place primary—if not sole—emphasis upon implementing laws and program standards to assure children's rights to protection and sustenance. This emphasis leaves the impression that that is the limit of the state's responsibilities.

Our position is that, whenever the state assumes the burden of placing children in residential care, its responsibilities extend far beyond protection and sustenance.

Children's Right to Achieve Basic Developmental Goals

In all cases where the state decides to assume responsibility for children, for a period of time or permanently, it implicitly asserts that it is more capable than the children's parents of child rearing. Thus, the state assumes obligations to assure children's rights to achieve developmental goals.

While parents are accorded wide latitude in defining what is appropriate developmental progress for their children and in selecting experiences that will promote their personal goals for them, the state is bound to far narrower limits in its definitions and experiential selections. Further, parents may for numerous reasons determine not to support the development of specific capacities evidenced by their children, while the state cannot do so without doing *de facto* harm to children's rights to achieve consistent with their abilities. Parents may, for example, choose not to support the musical, intellectual, or athletic talents of their children, but the state cannot exercise similar choices when assuming responsibility for these same children.

Thus, when the state places children in residential care, it must provide a programmatic approach that assure children's rights to achieve developmental goals consistent with their abilities. This approach must take the form of a case plan designed to assure each child's rights to individualization, socialization, and cognitive preparation that is initially fitted to, and is periodically updated to remain fitted to, the child's bio-social maturation level. Each of these three rights must be specifically addressed.

Individualization. All children have the right to develop a personal identity and a sense of self-respect. All children have the right to have some share of their daily experience given over for their sole use and benefit, the right to recognition of and respect for their unique characteristics, and the right not to be publicly labeled or made part of stigmatizing experiences.

To achieve this developmental goal, all children must have freedom of thought, expression, and bodily movement; privacy of thought, person, and personal possessions; latitude in decision making; recognition of personal achievements; opportunity to develop personal talents; and respect for family, cultural, and religious traditions.

Socialization. All children have the right to learn to understand, respect, and relate to others through interpersonal experience. All children have the right to have some share of their daily experiences given over to contact with other children and adults; the right to instruction in socially approved methods of behavior; the right to like or dislike whomever they please, so long as such decisions do not harm others; the right not to be purposefully excluded from contact with others on the basis of age, sex, income, culture, race, or similar criteria; and the right to access to their own families unless prohibited by judicial order.

To achieve this developmental goal, all children must be provided with free time and planned interpersonal and group experiences that encourage personal risk through give and take and trial and error. Personal risk must be encouraged by emphasizing that failure, even repeated failure, is a commonly experienced outcome in the process of achieving success.

This emphasis should shape the content and color the value of all social experiences, from instruction in table manners and modes of dress and address, through learning methods of group cooperation, to the formation of personal friendship, adult mentor, and dating relationships.

Cognitive Preparation. All children have the right to formal instruction to expand their understanding of themselves and the world and to prepare them for making their own livings, limited only by the demonstrated limits of their ability to learn. All children have the further right *not* to have their intellectual abilities prejudged or their futures hindered by the results of tests or evalutions.

To achieve this developmental goal, all children must be offered, among other things, a formal education in reading, writing, mathematics, and communication arts; special tutoring where required; opportunities to pursue talents or intellectual aptitudes; and appropriate vocational training.

We have purposefully stated that the core of the state's responsibility to children in residential care is this developmental goal in order to counter the all too common use of such placements as way stations where children mark time while having a rote list of their needs (not rights) attended to. While it may be possible for adults with intact personalities to be little affected by "serving time" in a prison, hospital, nursing home, or the like, this is not possible for children, who are, by definition, in a constant state of bio-social change. Children will change whether the fact of change serves as the basis for the services provided them in residential care or not. But if the fact of change is not recognized, their developmental progress may be distorted or retarded, no matter how handsomely their rights to protection and sustenance are met.

Children's Right to Corrective Intervention: Therapy and Control

A significant measure of how much the state honors the developmental perspective for serving children in residential care is the degree to which it places therapy and control interventions in the service of the overarching goal of developmental progress instead of letting them stand alone. No child can be well served in an environment that has as its basic emphasis either therapy or control. This is because both types of intervention are externally applied by adults with physical and intellectual power greater than that of the children and both are corrective, that is, they are applied after the fact to change or eliminate some condition. If emphasized as the core of a program of services, both can have the effect of encouraging dependency upon external authority among children, which is inimical to their development. Further, both approaches look backward toward something that has already occurred. The danger is that they can fix children in time by absorbing their energies in past-to-present reflection on pathology, thereby diverting them from present-to-future concerns.

Therapy. All children have the right to therapeutic intervention that corrects impediments to their developmental progress. Concomitantly, all children have the right to reject and have terminated any therapeutic intervention that cannot be demonstrated in clear and convincing fashion to be corrective. Following from this, every child has the right to have all therapuetic interventions monitored by a professionally competent, independent advocate.

To assure children's rights to therapeutic intervention, therapy itself must first be understood to be a time-limited activity designed to correct an existing personal problem or condition. To meet this definition, the following standards must be met, no matter what the proposed therapeutic intervention—chemical, mechanical, psychological, or social:

1. A specific problem must be identified by documenting the degree to which a child's condition or behavior deviates from that of other children of similar age and background.

2. Once a specific problematic condition or behavior has been identified, a convincing case must be made showing the problem to be an
impediment to developmental progress.

3. A goal must be set and a time limit imposed upon achieving the goal
via the intervention method selected.

4. The intervention method selected must conform to professional
ethics, be shown to be a preferable approach to the problem to be corrected, and be open to replication by other professionally competent persons.

5. The intervention must be terminated if the goal is achieved before
the imposed time limit or if the goal is not achieved by the end of the time
limit. Extensions of the time limit are warranted only when clear and
convincing progress can be documented by independent, professionally
competent judgment.

6. Records must be kept of all intervention episodes in such form that
will allow monitoring and evaluation of the therapeutic intervention by
independent, professionally competent persons.

These standards limit therapeutic interventions to specifically identifia-
ble personal problems or conditions. If these standards are not adhered
to, prospects increase that therapeutic interventions will be broadened
and applied to nonproblematic areas of children's conditions or behaviors, thereby turning their energies toward the correction of what are in
fact nonproblematic conditions or behaviors and increasing children's
dependency on external expertise over a greater portion of their daily life
circumstances.

From a developmental perspective, children cannot possibly benefit
from an extension of therapeutic intervention beyond the narrow confines
of the specifically identified problem. It would be difficult, if not impossible, to assure sufficient opportunity for developmental progress in an
environment that is oriented to pathology, so there is apparently no justification for "therapeutic milieu" residential care. Further, chemothera-
pies that have a general effect on behavior rather than a specific effect on a
specific personal problem or condition would be open to the same challenge.

Control. All children have the right to be controlled to prevent harm—
or the palpable threat of harm—to themselves or to other persons or their
possessions. All children have the right not to be controlled in any manner
that would jeopardize their physical well-being or in any manner that
reduces their freedom of thought, expression, or physical movement more
than necessary to prevent harm—or the palpable threat of harm—to

themselves or others. In addition, children have the right to prior knowledge of corrective methods and the behaviors to which they apply and have these monitored by a legally responsible, independent advocate.

To assure children's rights to control, control must be a time-limited intervention used to correct or prevent current harm to self or others. "Methods of control" as discussed here mean methods applied beyond those necessary to assure a child's rights to protection and sustenance. The exercise of control as a corrective mechanism is only justifiable if it relates to immediate events or situations. Imposing controls as a means of governing a child's general behavior, in response to an event that precipitated the need to exercise control, converts control to a form of punishment that is not justifiable from a developmental perspective.

To make the use of control beneficial to the developmental progress of children, the following standards must be honored:

1. The exercise of control is justifiable only as a response to an immediate event or situation that results in or poses a palpable threat of harm to children themselves or to others or their possessions.

2. Control may be exercised only in such manner and for the minimum amount of time needed to achieve an end to a harmful or threatening immediate situation or event.

3. Controls exercised to govern the future behavior of children in response to a specific event or situation must be justified in accord with the specific event or situation, time limited, and linked to a specific corrective end state (goal).

4. Controls exercised to govern the future behavior of children in response to a specific event or situation must be developmentally oriented, that is, they must allow children to earn their freedom from control through their own efforts. Controls that engage children in instruction and restitution are developmentally supportive; those that emphasize "serving time" in any manner are not and should be prohibited.

5. Controls are to be terminated at the end of imposed time limits, and time extensions are not warranted or justifiable.

6. Methods of control and the behaviors and situations governed by them must be set forth in writing and must be understandable to children in advance of their use.

7. All methods of control must fall within the limits of lawful and ethical behavior. All methods of control that cannot be documented to be for the primary benefit of the children exposed to them are prohibited, including all methods used by those who impose them for their personal

convenience, self-gratification, financial or other promotional gain, or exploitative purpose.

8. Records must be kept of all interventions that involve control in such a manner that they allow an independent, legally responsible person to judge their appropriateness.

These standards have as their purpose the bending of control interventions to the developmental benefit of children exposed to them. When control is placed in the service of overarching developmental goals, children are afforded opportunities to earn a restoration of their liberties at the earliest possible time through completing restitution or similarly constructive activities logically related to the situation or event that precipitated the need for control. This method fits controls to the specific event or situation and uses control as a corrective intervention.

Properly viewed, both control and therapeutic intervention are reactive in nature and episodic in implementation. That is, they are not used until circumstances occur warranting their use, and they are intended in practice to correct specific impediments to development. All control methods result, in one manner or another, in a suspension of personal liberties. The suspension of certain of a child's liberties regarding freedom of expression or action is, of course, justifiable when the child's behaviors lead to, or threaten to lead to, harm to the child or others. Control is, however, not justifiable solely on its own merits, because the suspension of a child's liberties can in no way, in and of itself, contribute to the continuation of the child's development.

Therefore, the placement of children in residential care for the primary reason of control is unjustifiable. Yet, many children classified as unruly, uncontrollable, deviant, and the like are placed precisely for control; and, in spite of the names ("treatment," "developmental," "correctional") by which the facilities in which they are placed like to be known, the core of service there fulfills the purpose of the placement, namely, control. When control assumes unwarranted importance by becoming the core rationale for a program of services, the tendency among those responsible for children in residential care is to begin to apply control to a broad range of child behaviors and situations that neither require nor warrant correction.

This use of excessive control teaches children that they have little control over themselves and little need to control themselves. This can easily lead to a reduction in risk taking or trial-and-error behavior as a means of evading restrictive reactions and an overall failure or fear-avoidance approach, rather than an achievement approach to living.

Residential placements that adopt control or therapeutic intervention as the core rationale for their service programs cannot, from a developmental perspective, assure the rights of children as we have presented them in this paper. They can only contribute to the distortion of children's developmental pathways and the retardation of their developmental progress, which at heart violates nearly everything to which children have rights. Rather, such emphases heighten the prospects of the children's withdrawal, hostility, and episodic bursts of self-destructive or otherwise aggressive behavior, which, put kindly, do not bode well for their achieving productive adult citizenship.

II. *State Responsibilities for Protecting Children in Residential Placements: Defining the Role of Child Protective Services*

Public concern is rapidly spreading beyond protecting children from abuse and neglect in the family and community to protecting them from institutional child abuse and neglect in other residential environments.[1] Commonly, a state's social service agency is assigned legal responsibility for receiving child abuse and neglect (CA/N) reports, performing investigations, reaching decisions, and, where needed, providing services to child victims and their families. These tasks, in turn, are normally delegated to the agency's CPS staff.

However, the tools available to CPS staff—as embodied in current state law, policy, or procedures—may be inadequate for coping with and preventing institutional child abuse and neglect. These shortcomings in existing statutes—and the policies and procedures that flow from them—stem from the fact that these laws were designed to enable CPS staff to cope with and prevent CA/N within the family and community, not in institutions.

This difference has begun to be recognized by states that require an independent agency to receive reports and investigate when CA/N is reported in residential placements operated or funded by the states' social services departments. Beyond this provision, however, CPS staff are left with the problem of having only a single set of tools to cope with and prevent CA/N in two grossly dissimilar environments.

---

[1]In this work the term "institutional child abuse and neglect (CA/N)" is restricted to acts or omissions committed or permitted to occur by responsible adults that are harmful to children in residential placements. Further, the term "residential placement" is limited to mean any institutional, group home, or foster family 24-hour child care facility over which the state has jurisdiction.

The following sections will attempt to clarify the distinctions between CA/N committed by parents or other ·citizens and that committed by agents of the state and to point out the implications of these distinctions.

Differences Between CA/N Identification Criteria in Homes and in Institutions

Because no law can set forth criteria that would be uniformly serviceable for identifying CA/N in all reports of incidents, the quality of CPS practice is governed more by the art of professional judgment than by scientific method or bureaucratic routine. Even the most precise criteria must be interpreted by CPS staff according to their feel for community standards and their awareness of the unique features of each case. CPS staff should—and probably already do—interpret existing criteria quite differently when applying them to cases of reported institutional CA/N. Indeed, these distinctions should probably be made explicit and incorporated into decision-making guidelines.

At least four distinctions are worthy of serious examination: the importance of degree of severity of impact on the child, the establishment of intent or purpose on the part of the adult, the degree of latitude allowed adults in justifying behaviors, and the range of adult behaviors determined to be permissible.

1. *Degree of severity*. When the alleged perpetrator of CA/N is a parent or other legal guardian, the CPS worker—and usually the juvenile judge—will want clear evidence that the adult acts or omissions under scrutiny have or will have harmful consequences for the child before even temporarily suspending and transferring parental rights to care for the child. Thus, when severity of impact cannot be documented satisfactorily, the CPS worker will often err on the side of the leniency.

The situation is radically different, however, for reports of institutional child abuse or neglect. For purposes of *determination*, when the alleged perpetrator is an agent of the state, severity of impact is irrelevant. Because an agent of the state has clearly accepted responsibility for carrying out state law, an act or omission in violation of the law is sufficient within itself to warrant a determination of CA/N, regardless of the immediate or future consequences for the child.

2. *Evidence in support of willful intent*. In the family/community environment, the CPS worker is faced with the difficult task of establishing motive or intent in arriving at a determination. Frequently, the line be-

tween intent and accident is hard to distinguish in physical abuse. It is no easier to fix a parent's direct contribution to a child's truant behavior or to determine neglect when a mother leaves her child with a neighbor for a prolonged period.

In material ways, the reverse holds true in investigations of institutional CA/N reports, primarily because children are in a residential facility for protective, developmental, and/or corrective reasons. Thus, even if physical harm is accidental, the agent of the state may be held accountable for not preventing the accident by providing a hazard-free enviroment. Similarly, establishing intent would not be necessary to determine neglect were an agent of the state to deposit a child with an unauthorized care giver for a prolonged period of time. Such a practice would constitute *de facto* neglect.

3. *Degree of latitude.* Standards for judging the quality of care provided by agents of the state to children in residential placements are less than precise. Nonetheless, they apply uniformly. That is to say, those responsible for children in residential placements are governed by broad community standards for the care and development of children, in addition to whatever codes of conduct a state explicitly sets forth.

On the other hand, parents and other legal guardians are allowed considerable latitude in deviating from these broad community standards (though not from legal prescriptions) on the grounds of personal preference, cultural and ethnic traditions, or family necessity. Parents, for example, may send their children to bed without supper as their personally preferred mode of discipline, may restrict their children from playing with children of another race on the basis of cultural beliefs, and may have several children sleep in the same bed because of economic necessity.

On what basis could an agent of the state justify similar behavior toward children?

4. *Range of behaviors permitted.* State law provides all children with certain protections from abuse and neglect, but the range of acceptable behaviors is far broader for parents and other legal guardians than for agents of the state. In addition to conforming to broad community standards for caring for and rearing children that may not apply to parents and the legal guaradians, agents of the state may be controlled and regulated by licensing standards, organizational and professional codes of ethics, and other procedural constraints. Physical discipline, for example, spanking and social isolation, may be permitted to parents but denied to agents of the state. Parents may inspect a child's personal mail, forego

needed dental work, allow siblings to occupy the same bedroom when one has a mildly contagious disease, and so on, while such practices by agents of the state may be prohibited.

Further, sibling and peer behavior are rarely judged by the same standards. As a consequence, adult responsibility for harmful interpersonnal acts among children differs for parents and agents of the state. Within limits, ganging up, fighting, and same or opposite sex exploration among siblings are dismissed as part of growing up, while similar behaviors among peers in residential placements are not condoned and those responsible for the care of such children are held responsible for preventing them.

When the aggregate effect of law, community standards, licensing standards, codes of conduct, and other procedural constraints is calculated, it is very clear that a far greater number of child caring and rearing practices are definable as abusive or neglectful when carried out by agents of the state.

In sum, a dual set of standards operates in practice—if not in law and policy—to guide the CPS worker in making determinations of child abuse or neglect: one for family/community environments and one for residential placements. Implicitly, agents of the state are held to stricter standards, and the CPS staff has less margin for exercising the benefit of the doubt in the investigation process. More often than in the family or community context, proof of the occurrence of an act or omission will be sufficient to a finding of abuse or neglect in a residential placement.

CPS Role in Preventing Abuse and Neglect

What is the extent of CPS and state social service agency responsibility in preventing abuse or neglect of child and family rights?

CPS responsibility extends from the decision to remove children from their homes through the termination of the state's involvement. It must be noted that the body of administration practices and program approaches used by a residential placement facility and its sponsoring state agency constitutes an additional potential source of child abuse or neglect, particularly as these practices and approaches affect the human, constitutional, and civil rights of children or their families. Failure to acknowledge these rights in the placement process or failure to document the rationale for making a placement decision can be *de facto* abuses on the part of the state agency. CPS staff have a role—albeit not an exclusive one—in protecting children from being harmed by their own practices and those of other agents of the state, while simultaneously protecting children from the harmful persons or circumstances that precipitated the need for removal and placement. Thus, for residential placements, CPS staff have protective responsibilities in two areas, namely, preplacement to placement, and administration and staff behavior while children are in placement.

First, CPS staff must avoid residential placement whenever possible and provide children with the least restrictive environment consistent with their needs.

In addition to safeguarding the rights of children and their families in the decision-making process, CPS staff must also be able to document clearly the need for removal from the home and be able to defend the appropriateness of the residential placement selected. For their part, residential placement facilities must clearly state the types of children they will accept and provide evidence of their capacities and qualifications for meeting the needs of those children. Those placement qualifications should be considered against the reasons for residential placement in the first place.

1. *Need for protection of person.* Is the residential facility free of environmental hazards? Are privacy of person and possessions assured? Do facilities, staff qualifications, and methods of supervision assure against physical intrusion or exploitation by peers, staff, visitors, or other adults? Is the location convenient to the child's home community, natural family, and other services?

2. *Need for basic care.* Are community standards adhered to in the provision of nutrition, clothing, preventive health care, and living space? Does the facility meet these standards for all residents uniformly? (In foster homes, do the foster care givers provide the same care as for themselves or their own children?)

3. *Need for developmental opportunities.* Does the residential facility provide children with appropriate educational, artistic, religious, recreational and social experiences, natural family contacts, and participation in planning?

4. *Need for correctional or specialized supportive services.* Can the residential facility meet the corrective or other physical, mental, or emotional needs of resident children? Are staff qualified to deliver special services directly (e.g., prosthetic fittings, physical therapy, chemical therapy, individual and group psychotherapy, special education) or to purchase and monitor these services from other sources?

The fact that some tests of appropriateness may not be included in current licensing standards and regulations does not relieve CPS from making sure that the residential placement resource is qualified and suitable. Sending a child into a placement of unknown merit may be on its face an abuse of the child's rights and may place the child at risk of further personal abuse or neglect, which, if it occurs, would be rightly traceable to CPS actions.

Secondly, CPS must also make sure that the child is protected while in placement. A facility may contribute to child abuse and neglect by failing to devise, promote, monitor, and enforce appropriate administrative practices and treatment approaches to govern the protection of residential children and the services provided them.

In a closed environment, administrative methods should protect resident children from harm. These methods should include:

1. Sound screening techniques to rule out job applicants with questionable credentials or work histories;

2. Effective measures for assuring the confidentiality of a child's records and the use of information in them by care-giving staff and other officials;

3. Promulgation of the residential facility's rules, codes of conduct, and rights and responsibilities to all staff, residential children, and families;

4. Operation of a human rights committee to review and authorize all treatment approaches;

5. Cooperation with a third party representing the child's interests (personal advocate, guardian, etc.) while in placement and assurance of mechanisms enabling the child to contact the representative in confidence whenever necessary.

Other methods should be added; this list merely points out that residential placements or their sponsoring state agencies must have administrative practices that protect a resident child's rights and person while in placement.

Administrative standards for staff behavior are needed to prevent arbitrary and capricious acts and to assure that staff behavior fufills the established goals. Such standards fall into three major categories:

1. *Standards for Uniformity*—It is an administrative responsibility to assure that all residential children are treated uniformly in protection of their rights and person, provision of their basic needs, adequacy of adult supervision, and case planning.

2. *Standards for Individualization*—To meet the needs of children as individuals, the administration must monitor the fit between case planning goals and the experiences provided by staff. A placement facility cannot argue failure to meet individual needs on the grounds of lack of resources.

3. *Standards of Fairness*—The sponsoring state agency and the residential placement facility must have behavioral standards governing the rights and responsibilities of staff and children relative to the limits of supervisory constraints; methods of discipline; discretion in personal care/demeanor; freedom of association with peers, family, and other outside contacts; choice in developmental opportunities; treatment approaches; and the like. The absence of such standards would increase prospects for arbitrary or capricious staff actions.

It is essential to have a mechanism for receiving and investigating reports of CA/N incidents independent from the residential facility in which they are alleged to have occcured. Most states are moving toward adoption of approaches that will satisfy this requirement. This does not, however, obviate the need for implementing internal mechanisms for monitoring care and staff behavior, for establishing a human rights review committee, for developing or cooperating with a third-party representative for each resident child, and for establishing confidential internal procedures for staff- and self-reporting of CA/N incidents.

Finally, the facility must clearly delineate the administrative role in the reporting-investigation-disposition process. The most useful standard for establishing the limits of internal involvement is that internal involvement should be terminated at the point where there is reasonable suspicion that current administrative practices (by their commission or omission) have contributed to the reported incident. Above all, determination of corrective actions should not be left with those who administer the residential facility. If adminstrative practices are clearly not implicated, a joint investigative role with the independent investigative agency recommending corrective actions should be used. When a staff member or caretaker is the sole perpetrator, administrative input about the perpetrator's employment record and potential for rehabilitation may be valuable. Clearly, however, when administrative practices are implicated, adminstrative participation in investigating and making recommendations should be ruled out.

Generally, the state social service agency and its CPS staff must assume more leadership in mandating standards for residential placement facilities under its authority and insisting upon their uniform application by the independent investigation agency and CPS staff alike when performing investigations.

III. *Some Steps for Improving the Reporting and Investigation of Child Abuse and Neglect in Residential Placements*

Existing state child abuse and neglect laws and the procedures that flow from them were designed to protect children within the family and community context and, as such, are not entirely suited to providing children in residential placements with equal protections. Yet states, through their mandated agencies, have a greater responsibility to assure the reporting of suspected incidences of child abuse and neglect in residential settings than within the family or community, because they have removed the children from their own families. They have the further responsibility for assuring that investigations of complaints occurring in placements under the auspices of the mandated agency will be carried out independent of that agency's influence.

Fulfilling these requirements is difficult, since there is such a bewildering array of residential placement facilities and licensing authorities. A state agency that is mandated to improve the reporting and investigation of child abuse and neglect in residential placements must deal with this bureaucratic muddle. The steps it takes must, therefore, be realistic. For example, the mandated state agency cannot be expected to provide a definitive list of abusive and neglectful behaviors, because observer and victim personal judgment will continue to determine whether making a report is justified or not. A list could only be a suggestion. In addition, licensing standards and codes, as well as the mandated state agency's criteria, will be used to warrant reporting.

What the mandated state agency can do is to guarantee everyone access to the reporting mechanisms, familiarize all pertinent persons with the mechanisms, and enforce compliance among all residential placement resources it operates or uses. This strategy would set an example so that, in the long run, other authorities responsible for residential placements would adopt similar reporting approaches and methods. These improved reporting approaches should maximize the reporting of suspicious incidents, thereby protecting children. Of course, the number of reports that prove to be unfounded may also increase.

Step 1. Increase public awareness. Public awareness campaigns in recent years have increased the number of CA/N reports. However, nearly all of these campaigns have aimed primarily at familiarizing the public with the occurrence of CA/N in the family and community context. Therefore, a first step is to tell the public that CA/N can and does occur in residential placements and that their responsibility to report, the immunity safeguards that guarantee them, and the penalties for nonreporting are the same as for occurrences in the family and community context. Current public awareness brochures could be cheaply revised to emphasize public reporting responsibilities relative to CA/N in residential placements.

Step 2. Educate the child's family. Families may be in confusion when their children are removed and placed, and parents or other legal responsible adult family members may not know what their continuing responsibilities are for the children in placement. Yet unless parental rights have been terminated, parents continue to have some responsibility to protect their children from abuse and neglect. The mandated state agency should inform family members of their continuing rights and responsibilities during the placement process. At minimum, parents should be told and given written material saying that they should report unusual occurrences that they notice in their contacts with their children.

Step 3. Train placement staff. The mandated state agency should provide written materials and instruction covering the state child abuse and neglect statute and individual responsibilities for reporting to every person providing care-giving services in residential placements that are used by the agency. This should be done when administrative personnel in group care settings are hired and when adoptive and foster families are licensed. A policy statement should be made that administrators in group care settings who receive reports from staff must immediately convey these reports to the mandated state agency and may not under any circumstance delay reporting while trying to resolve the matter internally.

Step 4. Improve mandated state agency staff reporting. The mandated agency receives reports on two types of children in residential placements: those who are placed under its auspices and those who are not. In the former case, most states obligate the agency to transmit the report immediately to the designated independent agency for investigation, but in the latter the agency can undertake the investigation itself. This approach should be pursued uniformly for children in all types of residential placements, including those in foster family homes. To avoid confusion and maintain consistency with state laws, the independent investigative agency should not have a separate, publicly distributed telephone number. Rather, the mandated state agency should continue to receive all calls and immediately transmit appropriate calls to the independent investigative agency. It may be hard to determine quickly whether the suspected victim is in placement under the agency's auspices or not, so an up-to-date listing of children placed under agency auspices should be available. These lists could be generated from intake, financial payments, or similar records routinely processed by the state agency or its local offices.

Step 5. Improve self-reporting. From the self-referral demonstration program in Knoxville, Tennessee, involving adolescent sexual abuse, we have learned that self-reporting is primarily dependent upon age, abilities, and access to reporting mechanisms. Children above the age of 10 with reasonable intelligence will use the telephone to self-report when they know of its availability and are assured of confidentiality. For handicapped children and those under the age of 10, this will probably not be a satisfactory approach to self-reporting. In short, a differential approach to self-reporting may offer the best prospects at the least expense. All placed children above age 10 with reasonable intelligence and each child under age 10 adjudged to have sufficient reasoning and communications skills should be counseled about what CA/N is, what their rights are, and how to report; all such children should be guaranteed immediate, unimpeded, and confidential access to a telephone, 24 hours a day, within the premises of the placement. In addition, every child in placement must have a legally responsible person appointed to perform monitoring and advocacy functions who makes periodic on-site contact with the child. In most cases the mandated agency's protective services staff can perform these functions. Indeed, these functions, along with coordination of service profession, can comprise the core of the caseworker's role in serving children in placement. To make this possible, however, each caseworker must be thoroughly trained in what is appropriate and inappropriate child protection, sustenance, development, and therapeutic and control intervention and must peform frequent on-site visits to assess these factors.

Steps for Improving the Investigation of Residential Child Abuse and Neglect

Investigations of reports of child abuse and neglect in residential placements differ qualitatively from those conducted in the family and community because no care giver—foster family, group home, or institution—has child-rearing rights equivalent to those of natural parents. Thus, extenuating circumstances such as personal choice, cultural beliefs, lack of funds, and the like are rarely—if ever—germane to the determination of whether CA/N occurred or not.

The investigations also differ because every placement is governed by an administrative authority, so the relationship between administrative acts of commission or omission to the reported event must be assessed. In group homes and institutions, an administrative authority is normally located on the premises. In the foster family home, the administrative authority is the placing agency that is currently using it. The need to assess the administrative contribution, if any, as a basis component of all investigations of reports of CA/N in residential placements justifies the establishment of an independent investigative agency to perform all investigations involving residential placements directly operated by the mandated agency. Unless this is done, administrators in the mandated state agency will be placed in the position of passing judgment upon themselves.

Thus, all investigations of reports of CA/N in residential placements must focus upon three basic questions.:

1. Did the reported event occur or not, independent of extenuating circumstances?

2. Is the administrative authority culpable or not, and if so, in what manner?

3. Is the problem, if validated, administratively redressable?

These questions imply that investigation of reports of CA/N in residential placements is a specialized matter that requires specialized knowledge on the part of those conducting them. In particular, investigators must be thoroughly conversant with a set of standards that is far stricter than that applied to investigations in the family/community context, and he/she must also have a sound working knowledge of administrative practices and organizational behavior to facilitate assessment of the role of the administrative authority in the reported occurrence.

The following steps could improve the investigative process:

Step 1. The mandated agency should adopt a written set of stricter standards by which reports of CA/N in residential settings will be judged and distribute it to all residential placement providers.

Step 2. The mandated state agency should limit the role of the administrative authority in the investigative process to full faith cooperation with investigative personnel. In effect, this policy would serve to prohibit the administrative authority from assuming responsibility for conducting the investigation and reaching dispositions itself.

Step 3. The mandated state agency should cooperate in the establishment of an independent investigative agency to fulfill the intent of the policy adopted by Step 2 and work to have its set of assessment standards adopted by the independent investigative agency to effect uniformity in investigative approaches.

Step 4. If an indepedent investigative agency exists, the mandated state agency should establish procedures to transmit appropriate reports to it immediately.

Step 5. The mandated state agency should appoint state-level staff to conduct investigations, provide them with identification credentials, and notify all residential placement providers in writing of their identity and role. A similar step should be taken by the independent investigative agency, accompanied by notification from the mandated state agency to its staff of the identity and roles of the independent agency's staff.

In our view, it is essential that investigative staff be of state-level authority to counterbalance and prevent intimidations by administrative authority, especially in powerfully connected, publicly and privately sponsored institutions.

Step 6. Investigative staff in the mandated state agency and in the independent investigative agency should receive special training in such areas as stricter standards of assessement, administrative practices, and organizational behavior, in preparation for carrying out the investigative role.

Step 7. Standards should be adopted governing the protection of the rights of alleged perpetrators during the investigative process. Among other things, these standards should protect alleged perpetrators from punitive administrative actions prior to an investigative finding and prevent authorities from making any personally accusatory entries into employment records, agency case records, or other official files or registries prior to a validated finding.

Step 8. Legal standards and procedures should be adopted governing the citing of validated instances of CA/N in letters of reference that administrative authorities provide for perpetrators who apply for work in child welfare and governing the use of the Central Registry for screening job applicants.

Step 9. The mandated state agency should establish a permanent committee composed of appointed agency staff and representatives from licensing authorities to distinguish licensing violations from other validated occurrences of abuse or neglect. This step would target dispositional actions toward administrative authorities, the perpetrator, or both and determine whether program or licensing authorities have responsibility for monitoring corrective interventions.

This committee should also develop a code of conduct to guide the behavior of all employees and volunteer care givers who provide services to children in residential settings. The code of conduct should be consistent with the set of standards adopted for assessment of reports.

Concluding Commentary

Taken together, these steps are more feasible than ideal. They do not constitute a "model," a logically consistent, inherently complementary total approach to reporting and investigating child abuse and neglect in residential placements.

Such an idealized total approach is, of course, easy enough to conjure up. It might, for example, take the form of a radical restructuring of state government by placing the mandated state agency at the pinnacle of authority and subordinating all other public and private residential placement programs and licensing authorities to it. Under this condition, most, if not all, existing bureaucratic entanglements, competing interests, duplications of effort, and questions of control would either evaporate or become much easier to manage. Since this is quite unlikely to occur, the mandated state agency must operate within a complex administrative milieu that will continue to influence the definition and limits of its role in the total reporting, investigative and dispositional process. Thus, the mandated agency can only adopt feasible steps and exercise leadership by example.

The aim of this paper has been to strike a mid-course between doing nothing and revolutionizing the system, both untenable options for a mandated state agency. A mid-course option is always much broader than those lying to either side. Thus, there is probably much more that could be done beyond what has been suggested here. Also, no particular mandated state agency will find a series of steps couched in general terms to be exactly fitted to its specific circumstances. Indeed, the aim of a mid-course approach is to stimulate expansion and adaptation of the material presented and, if this paper has that effect, the aim will have been met.

CORPORAL PUNISHMENT IN SCHOOL AS REPORTED IN NATIONWIDE NEWSPAPERS

Jacqueline Clarke
Rebecca Liberman-Lascoe
Irwin A. Hyman

ABSTRACT. The authors list the types of physical punishment used in the schools, the actions that cause them, and the responses to the punishments by students, communities, and parents. If parents object, the writers point out, they are more successful taking their complaints to the school board or administration than to court. Most of the information in the article comes from newspaper articles.

Corporal punishment still is a controversial issue in the United States. Only four states have banned its use—Hawaii, Maine, Massachusetts, and New Jersey. Maryland has limitations on its use, 12 states have remained silent on this issue, implicitly sanctioning the practice, and the remaining 33 states allow or specifically endorse the use of corporal punishment as a means of disciplining children within the schools (Hyman & McDowell, 1979).

Jacqueline Clarke, Rebecca Liberman-Lascoe, and Irwin A. Hyman are with the National Center for the Study of Corporal Punishment and Alternatives in the Schools, Temple University, 1801 Broad St., Philadelphia, PA 19122. The paper was presented at the annual convention of the National Association of School Psychologists, Washington, DC, April 10, 1980. It has been adapted by Ranae Hanson, editor of *Child and Youth Services*. Requests for reprints should be addressed to Irwin A. Hyman at the above address.

Fifty-eight cities within those states that allow its use have banned corporal punishment within their school districts. Baltimore, Chicago, the District of Columbia, New York City, and Pittsburgh are just a few examples (Lauscher, 1977). Many countries around the world have also banned the use of corporal punishment: Austria, Belgium, Cyprus, Denmark, Ecuador, Finland, France, Holland, Iceland, Israel, Italy, Japan, Jordan, Luxembourg, Mauritius, Norway, the Philippines, Qatar, Sweden, and all of the Communist bloc countries in Europe (Hyman & McDowell, 1979). Yet despite widespread disapproval of corporal punishment in schools, the American press is replete with the continuing saga of its use on children.

Students in American schools have been subjected to the use of the paddle, hand, rope, belt, and fist. In addition, they have had their hair cut off; been put in a storeroom, box, cloak room, closet, and school vault; been thrown against a wall, desk, and concrete pillar; been forced to run the "gauntlet" or "belt line"; been forced to do punishment push-ups; been stuck with a pin; had their mouth, hands, or body taped; been undressed in private or before peers; been made to stand on their toes for long periods of time; been punched; been dragged by the arm or hair; had meals withheld; been forced to stand in pajamas in 20-degree weather; been choked; been forced to lay on a wet shower floor in clothing; been made to eat cigarettes; been tied to a chair with a rope; and been forced to sit at a desk in a coat room with constant criticism.

All of these occurrences were reported since 1976 and were compiled by the newspaper clipping library at the National Center for the Study of Corporal Punishment and Alternatives in Schools.[1] Other practices may exist, but they have not been reported.

Ironically, the violent punishments described were meted out to students who in most cases had committed nonviolent acts. From a total of 343 violent punishments which had their reasons cited in the newspaper clippings, only 5.5% were used to discipline children who had committed

---

[1]This research paper encompasses only those articles purchased from Luce Press Clipping. The Center receives these articles from the End Violence Against the Next Generation, Inc. (EVAN-G) in California. The Luce Press Clipping service acquires newspapers from those publications which accept subscribers. It receives approximately 1800 dailies and 8000 weeklies from across the nation. The newspaper representation includes papers of liberal and conservative opinions, from large cities and small towns. This service conducted a study in August of 1978 to ascertain the percentage of newspaper articles located by their employees on a particular subject. The results of this study indicated that 80% of such articles were detected. All newspaper articles reported in this paper are located in the National Center for the Study of Corporal Punishment and Alternatives in the Schools.

violent acts. The violent acts which received violent penalties were fighting in school or on the school bus, pulling a chair out from under another student, and pushing another student down.

The majority of violations which received severe physical reprimands were of a nonviolent nature. The nonviolent acts included playing hooky from school or class; possessing cigarettes; smoking; misbehaving in the school hallway; coming to school or class late; not doing school work; getting poor grades; not getting test papers signed by parents; cheating on a test; remaining in the bathroom too long; writing a dirty word on the bathroom wall; running on school grounds; being in school hallway without a pass; kicking rocks against the school building; disrupting class; talking in class; accidentally hitting the principal's hand; chewing gum in school; being in school without permission; swearing; stealing a teacher's notebook, money, or master key; hitting a school bus with a tennis ball; lying; not having homework; standing in the school doorway, thus disturbing classes; parking on the school grass; throwing food; missing football practice; forgetting to raise one's hand; crying in school by a kindergarten child; and not pronouncing words correctly in a kindergarten phonics class.

Corporal punishment is the infliction of pain or loss of personal freedom for the commission of some offense. This infliction of pain is not limited to "paddling," which is performed with a wooden paddle, or of "spanking," which employs any other device such as a book, leather strap, or hand (Hyman, Bongiovanni, Friedman, & McDowell, 1977). Any excessive discomfort, such as forced standing for long periods of time or ingesting any substance foreign to the body, are included.

The general public maintains numerous misconceptions concerning discipline within the schools. They often think that the paddle is what is used to discipline children (Hyman & Wise, 1979), when, in fact, the paddle was only employed 66% of the time when corporal punishment was administered. Other methods of physical discipline were used in 34% of the cases.

Second, the size of the paddle is not standardized, as is often thought. The largest paddling instrument employed on a child was 3 inches wide, 1½ inches thick, and 24 inches long. Not only were the paddles of assorted dimensions, but so were the number of "swats" allotted to an individual child at one time for an offense. According to many school discipline codes, the accepted number of paddles for an infraction is a maximum of three to five "hits." Aside from the *Ingraham* v. *Wright* case (the first case about corporal punishment in the schools that the Supreme

Court agreed to hear), in which 20 and 50 "blows" were administered to the two boys, the greatest number of paddlings reported in the Center's newspaper library was 40 "smacks" to a Virginia youth.

Teachers are inconsistent in their reasons for punishing. One teacher paddled a child for talking in class but, at another time, did not paddle the same child for refusing to turn in a special work assignment without an accompanying explanation. Many teachers do not present classroom rules stating the type of punishment that will follow a misbehavior. Sometimes the paddlings are not for punishment. Celebrations, such as a birthday party, have included corporal punishment as a fun activity. This was not fun for a West Virginia sixth grader who received 12 to 14 blows with a paddle, although the ritual was once considered good-natured fun by the faculty.

The age and physical and mental health of the child are often not considered by the prosecuting adult. Children from 3 years of age to high school age have been corporally punished. Physical handicaps, blindness, or deafness have not deterred this type of punishment. Schools for students with emotional problems, retardation, and severe learning disabilities have used corporal punishment as a means of discipline. At one of these special schools, paddling was used extensively as a form of "motivation" for learning.

As another example, a 6-year-old child from Texas had suffered burns from a fire and had been hospitalized for 2 months as a result of the burns, which were listed as serious. After being released from the hospital, his mother put him back in his first-grade class. The staff was informed that the child had been put on medication producing drowsiness in order to ease the pain. Due to the medication's side effects, the child became drowsy and fell asleep in class. For this he was paddled by the school principal, regardless of the burns already on his buttocks and the fore-warning about the medication.

Moreover, corporal punishment can be imposed on many children at the same time. Examples include a physical education class of 50 students in Texas who received "licks" from a jumping rope for being noisy. In Florida, an entire class of sixth-grade boys were spanked when no one admitted to the writing of a dirty word on the wall of a freshly painted boys' bathroom. One hundred children in another Florida school were paddled for running on school grounds and the playground area. A ban on running had been imposed by the principal at this school because of several student injuries.

Not only do principals and teachers mete out corporal punishment to children, but so do other school personnel. A Texas janitor and an Alabama school bus driver physically abused children during the school day. In certain incidences, students performed the punishment. In South Carolina, the spanking of a student was inititated by the classroom teacher and partially administered by a fellow student. Another case in North Carolina involved one student who was forced to walk through a "belt line" consisting of older boys.

Football coaches are known for handing out the "whacks," especially to their athletic players. Three Dallas area high school football coaches have paddled athletes for unsatisfactory grades, poor attitude, and fighting in the locker room. They deal out the punishment based on a weekly grade and attitude report. The school superintendent accepts this as a "motivational device."

Many assume that corporal punishment is applied in private to the offending pupil with only two school personnel present—one to administer the punishment and the other to witness it. However, in one case a Texas vice principal paddled a youngster and broadcast the incident over the school's public address system for the other 850 students to hear. In Michigan an assistant principal, in search of a missing key, ordered 22 eighth graders to disrobe together in a gym locker room.

According to several newspapers, black and other minority youngsters receive a disproportionate number of physical punishments. The Florida *Sun-Sentinel* reported that in the Broward school system, blacks were paddled at the rate of 1 for every 6 students, whereas whites were paddled at a rate of 1 for every 14 students. At a Florida elementary school, black pupils accounted for 15% of the school's enrollment, yet 55% of those paddled were black. Sometimes the race of the punisher becomes the issue, as when a black Florida principal paddled every sixth-grade boy in the school after an investigation into the writing of an obscene word on the boys' bathroom proved inconclusive. When he was transferred to another school, black community leaders, colleagues of the principal, and parents questioned whether he was removed because of his race rather than because of the mass spanking. This case turned into a racial matter, with little attention paid to the children who were paddled.

Although some parents and doctors have specifically objected, either verbally or in writing, to physical punishment under any circumstances, many school officials choose not to respect their demands. In one such case, the school was informed that a certain child could not be paddled because he was dying from a blood disease, yet this same child was paddled hard and more than once for talking in class. A Mississippi doctor instructed the school not to physically punish his patient due to a "learning deficiency disease." The child was hit anyway. The mother of a Texas female student who was to accept a paddling for being tardy refused to permit male school officials to spank her daughter, so she took her protest to the school board. The community petitioned both pro and con, and the school trustees compromised with the mother, who agreed reluctantly to administer the spanking herself. Some recent court cases have ruled that schools may administer physical punishment, even in direct opposition to parents' wishes.

Communities do at times react to these practices in our schools. From the total 409 cases in the newspaper articles, 28% deal with community response to the use of corporal punishment. Most often the community seems either to be divided on the issue or to support corporal punishment. In Wisconsin a school adminstration and board tried several times to fire a principal who had a record of physically punishing students and who once allegedly broke a student's eardrum by striking the student. Each time the community protested the firing, finally by recalling five school board members and getting five other members on the board who would agree with them to keep the principal. When two Missouri boys developed medical problems after their high school principal had them eat cigarettes for punishment, their parents announced plans to sue the principal and school board; the parents reported that after that they received threatening letters and harassment from their neighbors.

It seems that parents of children in religious schools often defend personnel who use corporal punishment. In towns in Illinois, Wisconsin, and North Carolina, when suits were brought against ministers and principals of religious schools, the courtrooms were crowded with people supporting the defendants for paddling children.

Students themselves sometimes defend corporal punishment. In Arkansas a 16-year-old female was to be paddled for chewing gum in class. Eighty-three students signed a letter to the editor of the local paper approving the administration's decision to paddle her. In a North Carolina District Court, two teenagers who were indicted on charges of larceny for stealing $20 worth of gasoline and resisting arrest were allowed to choose their punishment: 5 days in jail or a paddling. Both chose the paddling. In several instances a child was given the choice between physical punishment, such as paddling, or nonviolent forms of discipline, such as suspension or detention, and chose the physical punishment.

Other times students violently reject physical punishment. A 13-year-old Oklahoma student took the board he had been paddled with and hit the principal over the head, causing a cut that had to be closed with four stitches. In Pennsylvania, a 13-year-old girl slapped her teacher after being paddled. In Alabama, a 13-year-old boy who had been paddled returned with a gun and shot the principal.

Sometimes family members too react violently. After a Texas elementary school custodian spanked a student, the child's grandmother confronted him, argued with him, and fatally shot him. To "show them what it felt like,"a Georgia father struck a principal with the paddle the principal had used to paddle the man's son. The father sued the principal, and the principal sued the father. After a 10-year-old Tennessee boy was paddled, his parents and sister came to school to confront the teacher, and the father hit the teacher. Warrants were filed against the father and sister, and the parents filed for a warrant against the teacher.

Instead of reacting violently, parents more frequently bring suit to court or complaints to the school board about the corporal punishment administered to their children. In these newspaper articles, the use of excessive force was the reason for 88% of the complaints; another 3.9% of the parents claimed that the school had neglected to notify them before or after the child received corporal punishment; 3.9% protested the administration of the punishment in the presence of other pupils; 2.2% alleged that a second adult was not present to witness the acts; 1.3% maintained that the punishment was performed in anger; .4% stated that corporal punishment was administered after the parents had objected to the use of physical force as a means of discipline for their children. Excessive force brought the greatest number of complaints, probably because extreme force often results in more lasting pain and evidence. Without welts, bruises, cuts, or broken bones to make the incident apparent, children tend to avoid telling their parents of their misdeeds for fear that they will be punished at home as well. Unless they are told, the parents will not be able to protest the incident.

In these newspaper stories, 47 parents were reported to have brought suit to court; 6 were successful. On the other hand, 56 cases were brought to the school administration or school board, and 34 were successful.

Parents or students who wish to resolve their complaints concerning corporal punishment will tend to be more successful with their local school administration or school board than with the court system. A chi square test was completed to compare the difference in success with the court versus the success with the school administration or school board.

The chi square indicates that there were significantly better results ($\chi^2 =$ 9.8, $p < .01$) for parents who went to the school administration or school board rather than to the court. Thirteen percent were successful in resolving their cases in court, whereas 60% of those bringing their complaints to the school administration or school board found satisfaction.

At times the school administration and the courts have not agreed. A North Carolina court acquitted a teacher on charges of an alleged corporal punishment complaint, but the local school board voted that the circumstances warranted the teacher's being fired. The data suggest that the possible elected status of individuals on the school board make them amenable to community opinion, whereas the judicial system must comply with the precedence of cases relating to this issue.

When school personnel were penalized, the school adminstration tended to impose reprimands more frequently than the courts. School administrations have taken no action, demanded a promise from the offender that such an action would not be repeated, placed a written reprimand in the mailbox or personnel file, warned that such an offense should not occur again, transferred the offender to another school or job within the district, suspended the transgressor for a number of days with pay or without pay, and dismissed the offender. Penalties imposed by the court have included probation, supervision, and payment of monetary damages.

Subsequent to complaints or court suits, many school districts have adopted written discipline codes. The codes of many districts cited in the articles tend to be similar: the presence of school administration or teaching staff to witness and administer the punishment is required; that is, the reprimand must not occur in the presence of other students; the punishment must not be administered unreasonably, excessively, or in the heat of anger; and finally, it should only be used as a "last resort" after all other physical efforts have been exhausted. Recent additions have included the notification of or written permission from the child's parent. Another requirement includes recording or processing a written report of the incident, as well as listing all attempts to resolve the behavior problem before corporal punishment was applied. The use of physical force is permitted in the protection of one's self or another, in the restraint of a student from hurting himself/herself, and for the protection of school property. In an effort to inform students and parents of their rights, school districts are attempting to disseminate written information on this subject. Yet too often these codes are not stated in school policies.

Most psychologists agree that corporal punishment is detrimental to the development of a child (Hyman & Wise, 1979). Yet the acceptance of

corporal punishment has pervaded all aspects of our society
school boards, and doctors have implicitly sanctioned its use at ti
Supreme Court ruling seems to be encouraging its use. Yet if
punishment is legally accessible to teachers, then why is it a taboo
Why are teachers not told how, when, where, and why to use
penalized for administering it incorrectly? If teachers and admini
had procedures to follow in administering discipline, parents and
boards would not have to spend so much time and money investi
complaining, or suing. Teachers would know what type of disciplir
could use and would not fear being brought to court, reprimande(
pended, or fired.

Discipline is a serious school problem today. We do not believe i
use of corporal punishment, but if it is going to be used, clear, wi
policies on when it is appropriate and what methods are condoned sk
be explicitly stated by school boards, including the rights of chil(
parents, and teachers. The critical issue is justice for children. Hui
rights should not be limited only to adults.

REFERENCES

Hyman, I., Bongiovanni, A., Friedman, R. H., & McDowell, E. Paddling, punishing and
   force: Where do we go from here? *Children Today*, 1977, *6*, 17-23.
Hyman, I., & McDowell, E. An overview. In I. A. Hyman & J. H. Wise (Eds.), *Corporal*
   punishment in American education. Philadelphia: Temple University Press, 1979.
Hyman, I., & Wise, T. (Eds.). *Corporal punishment in American education.* Philadelphia
   Temple University Press, 1979.
Lauscher, S. *Corporal punishment in public schools: The constitutional arguments.* Unpub
   lished doctoral thesis, George Washington University, 1977.

RELIGIOUS VALUES AND CHILD ABUSE

Adah Maurer

ABSTRACT. The writer tells of pressure by some religious groups to use corporal punishment in child care centers. She presents methods of countering such arguments.

When Christianity is practiced as a religion that understands God to be authoritarian and violent it may thus contribute to violence. Mainstream Christianity presents a God who is understood, reinterpreted and fulfilled in Jesus as the God of Love.

On Being a Child
United Presbyterian Church
Commission on the International Year of the Child

"But what about the Bible? What about 'Spare the rod and spoil the child'?"

Her child lay near death in the hospital. She had sobbed out her remorse, her shame, her embarrassment, and now in the forgiving silence after the policeman had gone, alone with a sisterly woman who seemed willing to listen, she could blurt out some justification for what she had done. "What about the Bible?"

The social worker did not answer the question. The harassed young mother had more immediate needs than an exegetical disquisition on a religious text. Arrangements had to be made to set up a medical appointment, to get food in the house, to begin counseling. The subject did not come up again, but it was not forgotten. For the social worker it lay heavily, like an indigestible lump that must someday be dealt with and examined.

Religion for a great many educated people is a pleasant, friendly back-

Adah Maurer is Executive Director of End Violence Against the Next Generation, Inc., 977 Keeler Avenue, Berkeley, CA 94708. Requests for reprints should be addressed to Adah Maurer at that address.

57

ground, a nostalgic feeling for childhood friends who listened enthralled to Bible stories. The Ten Commandments and the Golden Rule have been absorbed into a matrix of ethical actions scarcely distinguishable from the Bill of Rights and one's personal experience. It is a pleasant ambience that is ignored as air is ignored, except in a storm or when polluted. And the stormy question, "What about the Bible?" asked angrily, belligerently, or defiantly, as a rationalization for child abuse, seems alien, even sacrilegious. Yet for one's own peace of mind, there ought to be some way to deny that the Bible condones, much less advises, beating babies. Is "spare the rod" really there?

The question has greater than personal importance. When church-related groups want the right to use spanking in their own nursery schools, they attack state regulations that forbid corporal punishment. In Texas, where a great many child care facilities are sponsored by churches, some of the church-run facilities made headlines with noisy claims that any prohibition or even limitation on physical punishment is contrary to their religious beliefs. The matter of discipline, in their opinion, is part of the whole issue of separation of church and state, so all such regulations are an infringement on their religious liberty. Yet one Texas string of homes for wayward girls made another set of national headlines when escapees described the shocking punishments they had endured. To try to bridge the gap in opinions, the Texas Department of Human Resources set up a Church Relations Advisory Group, and so far state standards have prevailed. In day care, no child under 5 years of age may be spanked, and residential treatment centers for the mentally retarded and the emotionally disturbed, as well as emergency shelters and the like, are prohibited from shaking, striking, or spanking.

At the behest of Baptist Fundamentalist groups, the Iowa legislature adopted a bill permitting spanking in state-run nursery schools; then, because others protested, it amended the law to permit parental choice, hoping that the change would satisfy everyone. It did not. Parents who prefer to gentle their infants into civility prefer that the nursery schools not be half slave and half free. If some are spanked and howl their protest, they feel that the air will be blue with recrimination—the atmosphere one of distrust and fear. It would also be unfair when two little ones are learning to share that one should be walloped and the other have "taking turns" explained in courteous tones. Norm Ostbloom of the Polk County Social Service Department published in the *Des Moines Register* a searing statment that said in part:

Amidst all the verbiage about parents' "right" to have their preschool children corporally punished in day care centers, an important point has been missed. What about the rights of parents who don't want their children exposed to these violent methods of dealing with problems?

Advocates state that spanking young children will keep them out of prison, but research reveals just the opposite. Nearly all prisoners were corporally punished as chidren. . .

Such opinions, along with intensive lobbying by moderate groups, turned the tide, so spanking in nursery schools and foster homes is not permitted in Iowa.

In California, corporal punishment, with or without parental permission, has been forbidden in all child care facilities from foster homes to juvenile detention camps since the 1930s. Only recently has this position been questioned by Orange County fundamentalist groups. In the same manner as in other states and at the urging of the same ultrareactionary radio preachers, the religious "right" to spank children in church-run nursery schools is being demanded, thus far without success, but at considerable cost in time, energy, and funds.

In some other states, courts have imposed the limitations on physical punishment in institutions. In South Carolina in 1978, Judge William J. Craine, Jr., of the Family Court of the Eighth Judicial Circuit in Newberry, ruled that Jeff Bedenbaugh, who was then 10 months of age, had been recklessly punished. The infant boy had been enrolled in the day care program of the Independent Bible Baptist Church School of Prosperity, South Carolina. He had been sick for 3 weeks, and on the first day that his mother returned him, he cried during most of the day. In an effort to stop this "attention seeking," the head of the school, Charles Sprowls, gave Jeff—in Spowls' words—"cracks" on the butt. When the attention seeking did not stop, Jeff was spanked three times more. A witness said that when his mother came to get him, the marks on his bottom were "like ink-stains."

The Newberry County Department of Social Services entered suit to close the school and to prevent Mr. Sprowls from operating any day care facility in the state. In his defense, Sprowls said that his was a fundamentalist school. His religious conviction was that corporal punishment is necessary in child rearing to beat the evil that is born in children out of them. Further, he argued that since the First Amendment to the Constitution guarantees religious liberty ("Congress shall make no law respecting the establishment of a religion, or prohibiting the free exercise thereof. . . .") any restriction on his spanking baby Jeff would be unconstitutional.

In rebuttal, Dr. Eli Newberger, Director of Family Development Study of Children's Hospital Medical Center of Boston, testified that baby Jeff had been exposed to substantial risk of permanent injury and that the seven "cracks" he had received could have resulted in a broken spine, rendering the infant paraplegic in a fatal hematoma of the abdomen or in a ruptured spleen.

In the case of Sprowls, Judge Craine decided that spanking the infant not yet 1 year old had been reckless rather than reasonable, since a child that young obviously could not understand the purpose of the punishment. In his official statement, Judge Craine wrote, "I find that an individual may believe what he wishes; however, the state has a legitimate interest to protect its children from child abuse." Restraining this type of punishment "violates no first amendment privilege," he wrote, and he quoted eight other cases, including an 1878 bigamy conviction, where exemptions from laws had been claimed on religious grounds and had been denied.

More recently, possible dangers of such "religious rights" proved true when Jaja Chainey was beaten to death, not by a murderous or psychotic parent, but by a North Philadelphia religious leader who gave the 4-year-old religious chastisement for being inattentive to a reading lesson. The Reverend Darryl Justic Forrester was ordered to stand trial for murder; bail was set at $100,000, in spite of Forrester's plea that he had not meant to really hurt the boy.

Religious freedom is thus not absolute. If a religious group should attempt to revive human sacrifice—once a consecrated ceremony, as when Abraham was willing to offer up his son Isaac as a burnt offering to the glory of the biblical Jehovah—no claims of religious rites being freely exercised would be upheld. American justice would play the role of the angel who stopped the sacrifice saying, "Lay not thine hand upon the lad, neither do thou anything unto him."

With the emergence of a newly vocal element calling itself the "moral majority," these questions of church/state jurisdiction are certain to make headlines in the coming months and years. Although questions of abortion and pornography will be given greater visibility, local bickering about physical punishment of children may explode into a major issue. It is perhaps wise, therefore, for child care workers to be prepared to face down an irrational onslaught of pseudopious child assault situations.

Very little research has been done on the characteristics of people whose predominant mode, including their religious outlook, is punitive. In 1964, *Child Development* reported on a study of 360 families in Tennessee which found that those families who used threats that God would punish the disobedient child were more often low income; lacking in affection; demanding of conformity to unquestioned authority; and containing weak, powerless, and ineffectual personalities. More recent studies of child abusive families have painted the same picture. It seems that attitudes about a punishing God correlate with potential child abuse.

One must note that not all Christian denominations subscribe to these punitive sentiments. Not even all Funadmentalist sects agree. An issue of *Plain Truth*, in which the first two articles were devoted to proving that evolution could not have happened by chance and extolling the truth of the biblical story of creation, featured a cover-story article deploring child abuse and recommending nonviolent child rearing. "Of course children should honor their parents," it explained, "but inherent in the principle is the responsibility of those parents to behave honorably." Instead of reiterating the "inherent evil" philosophy, it emphasized the biblical commandment "Fathers provoke not your children."

During the International Year of the Child, the Presbyterian Church published and recommended for study and action the booklet *On Being a Child*, which makes a strong case for nonviolence. "An end to corporal punishment at home, in schools and in the justice system is important if violence [in our society] is to be suppressed," it said.

The Catholic Church in many communities is leading the way in abolishing corporal punishment in their schools, yet they are just as split on the present day applications of the concept of original sin as their Protestant counterparts. In 1978, the *U.S. Catholic* published the article "People Are Not For Hitting" by John Valusek, along with 60 comments from readers. The comments were split three ways. About a third of the letter writers agreed with Valusek that spanking children is unwise; another third screamed fire and brimstone if children's evil nature should be permitted to run wild; the last third wrote, "Yes, but . . ." The American people as a whole were probably split the same way in the 1970s. The trend as the 1980s begin seems to be toward greater divergence between more strongly held antithetical opinions.

Yet, it is futile to argue religion. People may be drawn to one sect or another, depending upon their emotional needs. Those who are fearful, uncertain, powerless, and who yearn for strong leadership, positive dogma, lack of ambiguity, and revenge on their persecutors, real and imaginary, may cling to a talisman as a neglected baby clings to a teddy bear. The Bible as immutable truth seems a safe, solid rock to which they can cling in the storm. They may rarely actually read the Bible, but they absorb some emotional strength from believing in it and quoting a few well-worn phrases from it. They do not tolerate debate about it. The social worker I mentioned at the beginning was wiser than she knew in refusing to discuss with the guilty mother her rhetorical question, "What about the Bible? What about 'Spare the rod and spoil the child'?" Benign silence and the action of refusing to further punish the mother, but instead ministering to her needs, spoke louder than words.

For the secure however, it is interesting to recognize that the historical trend, with some backsliding, has been toward greater compassion, more caring, and less cruelty toward children. If present day child abuse seems to belie this, consider Hansel and Gretel, the Children's Crusade, the London lives that Dickens described. Read Lloyd DeMause's *History of Childhood* and David Bakan's *Slaughter of the Innocents*. In the Bible this increase in tolerance is apparent too. Read again the story of the Akeda: Abraham and the Jehovah that he served who demanded willingness to kill the most precious first-born son (Genesis 22:1-13). Then when you read Proverbs, about which the punishers are so adamant, you will recognize that "Withhold not correction from the child: for if thou beatest him with the rod he shall not die" (Proverbs 23:13) is a compassionate improvement over burning the child.

Over its history the United States has also moved toward greater gentleness. The cruel and unusual punishments forbidden by the Eighth Amendment to the Constitution originally referred to drawing and quartering and breaking on the wrack, the excruciating tortures that our ancestors invented to punish heretics, witches, and other dissidents. Now it refers to such things as pumping out the stomach of a suspect who might have swallowed the evidence. In spite of many pockets of cultural lag, our world is an easier, more comfortable, less hurtful world than ever existed before. We have a long way to go, and there are those who would pull us back into viciousness, but the overall trend is unmistakably benign.

We know that the best way to defuse an angry child is to tell him something nice about himself. This ought to work as well with the Bible Thumpers, who do have points with which we can agree. I, myself, have at least one thing in common with the "moral majority": I much prefer "60

Minutes" to "The Dukes of Hazard." If their efforts result in less sex and violence in the entertainment offered us, that is all to the good. Perhaps we can also help them sheath the "Sword of the Lord" instead of brandishing it before the next generation.

INSTITUTIONAL NEGLECT OF
JUVENILE HEALTH NEEDS

David J. Berkman
R. W. Lippold

ABSTRACT. This section speaks of the health needs of juveniles who enter the
juvenile justice system. It points out that these health problems may have strongly
contributed to the problem behavior but that they are rarely treated in the institutions.

Although it can be anticipated, based upon national health statistics,
that juveniles entering or coming into contact with the juvenile justice
system either as dependent and neglected children or alleged or adjudicat-
ed juvenile offenders would be in need of medical care, information is
scarce as to the types and incidence of these medical needs.

National health statistics indicate that certain groups of lower socioeconomic juveniles have a greater number of unmet health needs. In
addition, national statistics on juveniles entering or coming into contact
with the juvenile justice system indicate that juveniles entering are often
disproportionately from lower socioeconomic and minority groups.

This article is from the *Juvenile Justice System Processing and the Disposition of Juveniles
with Special Problems*, a working draft by David J. Berkman and Charles P. Smith, submit-
ted to the National Institute for Juvenile Justice and Delinquency Prevention, December
1979, by the National Juvenile Justice Assessment Center of the American Justice Institute,
1007 7th St., Sacramento, CA 95814. This section is from "Medical Problems" (pp. 8-15,
18-22, 90, 92) by David J. Berkman and R. W. Lippold.

Therefore, it can be anticipated that delinquent, status offenders, and dependent and neglected juveniles will have greater health care needs than the general juvenile population. Even without attributing the health problems of juveniles as a causal or contributing factor (which they may be in some cases) to their delinquent or status offender behavior, there is sufficient evidence to suggest that special attention should be given to this relationship, as well as justifying a concerted effort toward meeting the greater medical needs of this population.

One study indicates that delinquent juveniles have a greater need for continual medical care during childhood and adolescence than nondelinquent juveniles, especially in relation to physical traumas due to accidents or injuries. The clinical observation of high incidence of multiple accidents, injuries, and illnesses among juveniles referred to a juvenile court clinic stimulated a study of the hospital records of 109 delinquent children compared with a matched comparison of 109 nondelinquents. Dr. Dorothy O. Lewis, a clinical professor of psychiatry at the Child Study Center of Yale University, observed that many of the court referrals to the clinic had been hit by cars, fallen from roofs, or suffered serious physical trauma at the hands of relatives and peers. Suspecting that some of these injuries and illnesses may have contributed to their delinquent behavior by reducing the juveniles' ability to form appropriate judgments, assess reality, or control their behavior, Lewis examined the incidences of injury and illnesses among the delinquent referrals as compared with those of nondelinquents in the sample population. Based upon an evaluation of the medical history of each juvenile in the sample, it was found that:

—Delinquent juveniles were far more likely than nondelinquent juveniles to be seen for accidents (particularly head or face trauma).
—Delinquent juveniles made significantly more hospital visits than did nondelinquents (especially before age 4 and between ages 14 and 19) (Lewis & Shanok, 1979, p. 1020).

Therefore, the results of this study suggest that delinquent juveniles have significantly more hospital contacts and significantly more accidents and injuries throughout childhood than do nondelinquent children. The implications of these findings are significant for the prevention of serious delinquency. According to Lewis, a history of frequent hospital contacts in the absence of a single medical disorder (e.g., asthma) should be a signal to the possibility of associated delinquent behavior and severe intrafamilial disturbance (Lewis & Shanok, 1979, p. 1024).

Probably the first major point in the juvenile justice system process at which juveniles are examined for medical problems is the intake examinations following admission into juvenile detention. For many of these juveniles, the medical examinations at detention intake represents the first thorough examination since infancy. Dr. Iris F. Litt of the Division of Adolescent Medicine at Montefiore Hospital in Bronx, New York, studied the needs uncovered during thorough intake examinations of 31,000 juveniles aged 8 to 18 admitted to the New York City detention facilities over a five-year period. Dr. Litt found that approximately 50% of the "healthy-appearing" juveniles admitted for detention were found to have physical illness, exclusive of dental or psychiatric problems (Brecher & Della Penna, 1975, p. 35). According to Litt:

> These health problems generally fall into three categories: First, those common to all adolescents during the period of rapid growth and body change that is the essence of adolescence. In this category are the orthopedic, gynecologic, endocrinologic and dermatologic conditions which plague teenagers of all socio-economic backgrounds. The second category is that which encompasses the medical or physical complications of the lifestyle of some adolescent patients and includes venereal disease, unwed pregnancy, and complications of drug abuse. Four and one-half percent of the girls, with an average age of 14.5 years, were found to be pregnant at the time of admission. Most were previously unaware of their pregnancy, and none had used any form of contraception. One-third of the adolescents admitted to the facility have been found to be users of drugs. On the basis of screening liver function tests on those drug users who had no symptoms of hepatitis and who had negative physical examinations, 39% or 3,700 were found to have a form of hepatitis. The third large category of illness included those usually discovered at an earlier age but, because of the pattern of poor medical care available to the youngster's families, were not detected until the time of their examination at the center. Congenital abnormalities, ranging in severity from heart disease, kidney and endocrine defects, to hernias requiring surgery make up the bulk of this category. The majority of these defects could have been corrected surgically at a younger age, at a lesser cost to the patient and to society. In some cases, the presence of these defects may have actually contributed to the youngster's school difficulty with resultant truant behavior, and many have, in fact, been a factor in their difficulty with the law (Brecher & Della Penna, 1974, pp. 35-36).

Dr. Litt points out that medical consideration must be given to whether incarceration in an institution may effect disruption in pathophysiology as in diabetes, asthma, peptic ulcer, and epilepsy, as well as complicate the differential diagnosis of amenorrhea (absence or suppression of menstruation). Generally, her experience with youth detention facilities has shown that, although the detained population may suffer from pre-existing poor health by virtue of lack of medical care prior to detention, or as by-products of the lifestyle of those who eventually become imprisoned, certain conditions can become exacerbated by incarceration or developed during the period of incarceration (Brecher & Della Penna, 1974, p. 35).

A similar study conducted by the Norfolk Health Department in 1972 of juveniles detained during a seven-month period in the Norfolk juvenile detention center indicated a high incidence of medical problems and a low rate of referral or treatment for identified medical problems. A review of 296 juvenile health records during this period indicated 331 separate health problems. Of the 331 health problems identified, 71% remained untreated (Kosidlak, 1976, p. 96). The majority of health problems identified were dental (27%), skin (23%) and throat infections (10%). The following types of cases had a better than 50% rate of treatment or referral: identified breast mass, convulsions, emotional or mental disorders, venereal disease, throat infections, and cases which required family planning (e.g., contraception). However, the majority of the identified cases were not treated or referred to a community health service resource.

The data on referral or treatment suggest that the detention facility was caring for health problems which were of an emergency nature, while neglecting those not requiring immediate attention during the period of detention. It is unfortunate that adequate provision was not made for community referral of identified health problems which remained untreated in the detention center.

As pointed out earlier by Dr. Litt, in addition to preoccurring medical problems, many medical problems observed during detention develop either during arrest or during the period of detention. Dr. John Carper, Director of Ambulatory Pediatrics, Boston City Hospital, reports that among a population of delinquent boys in a detention center with a daily census of 100 and an average stay of six days, several types of traumas are observed which probably develop during arrest or detention, and which make up about 25% of the cases seen during sick call:

Frequently seen are median nerve injury produced by handcuff trauma resulting in weakness, pain, and paresthesia to the thenar eminence. Severely swollen knuckles are sometimes seen sporadically on examination of a very angry frustrated boy who has been hitting his fist against the wall. At other times there are brief episodes of painful knuckles caused by the winner of a card game striking the narrow end of a deck of cards against the knuckles of his opponent. Multiple cigarette branding marks over the volar aspect of the forearm is commonly seen, caused by a peculiar kind of "chicken" game played by a pair of boys. Two boys were seen recently with linear third degree burns, 8 cm. long, on the dorsum of the right arm of one and of the left arm of the other. The burns resulted when the boys had allowed 20 cigarettes to burn out consecutively in the crease formed by holding their arms together before conceding the contest a draw. Multiple superficial transverse cuts and scars on the forearm are not infrequent and represent self-mutilation and suicidal gesturing. Resolution of intepersonal differences in a group of inarticulate boys is usually physical and accounts for many of the lacerations, sprains, broken noses, and traumatic injuries to the mouth, eye, teeth, and extremities (Carper, 1974, pp. 209-210).

In addition to arrest and assaultive and self-afflicted traumas, Dr. Carper also observed during daily sick call that approximately 50% of the boys have respiratory infections, gastrointestinal complaints, or skin problems, and 20% have some type of emotional adjustment problem which may include drug abuse.

It was also observed that some psychological adjustment problems of adolescents in a detention center take on physical symptoms. Many of these psychological problems masquerade as medical problems with symptoms of chest or abdominal pains, although they may be due to the anxiety brought on by detention. Based upon findings of two surveys conducted on problems on sick call, a few juveniles may actually account for a large percentage of the total daily sick call. Dr. Carper suggests that these problems can be best managed by listening to the juvenile after doing a careful physical examination and then providing reassurance. Many detained juveniles, although initially frightened, hostile, or depressed, respond well to medical personnel who show interest in and concern for them, and who can remain detached from the fact that these juveniles have been commited for delinquency.

Dr. Carper points out that the most serious defect uncovered in his review of detention medical care was not a physical one, but a monumental defect in the health care system in general.

Boys needing consultation, based on our findings, were not referred in a systematic way to a specialist or hospital. Only casually were any boys referred, because no referral mechanism had been established between the Department of Youth Services and a secondary or tertiary health care program. Thus, much of the effort and purpose of screening for defects was negated (Carper, 1974, p. 213).

This finding supports the need for coordinating medical care resources within the detention facility with those in the community. While it may not be practical or always feasible to meet all medical needs of detained juveniles within the facility due to the shortness of detention or the limited resources of the facility, it is possible and necessary for the detention facility to develop the mechanisms of systematic referral and the required cooperation for follow-up medical care in the community upon release, or within other programs or institutions upon the transferral of the juvenile. Without referral or follow-up, the health problem may remain untreated, thereby possibly developing into serious medical complications, or continuing to affect the ability of the juvenile to function in the community.

In some ways, institutionalized females have unique medical problems. Dr. Hania W. Ris, in a paper discussing her ten-year experience as medical director of the Wisconsin School for Girls, found that the great variety of health problems found among the female population included:

Acne and other skin disorders, gonorrhea, vaginitis due to trichonomas and yeast infection, menstrual dysfunction, out of wedlock pregnancy, obesity, suicide attempts, headaches, abdominal pain, hearing defect, refractory errors, conversion neurosis, self-mutilation in the form of "carving" (self-inflicted cuts), and cigarette burns, tatooing, traumatic injuries, learning problems, and drug abuse (Ris, n.d., p. 228).

Problems related to certain venereal disease, pregnancy, and abortion, as well as general menstrual problems, are prevalent among institutionalized females (see Ris & Dodge, 1972, 1973).

In some facilities, a major need for readily available abortions for those girls who choose them as an alternative to unwanted pregnancy exists. Dr. Ris notes that after a program was established in the new School for Girls and known to parole officers in the State, a few girls were actually admitted to the institution for the sole purpose of obtaining an abortion.

It was and still is easier to arrange an abortion for our young, alienated, poor youth through our facilities than in our own communities. It is an indictment of our society that a child has to be admitted to a correctional institution with a quality medical program to get adequate medical care (Ris, n.d., p. 228).

The lack of community alternatives for female juveniles focusing on difficulties in the home, school, or problems related to health contributes in large measure to the apparent size of the female delinquency problem. Female delinquents are institutionalized more often than males, for less serious crimes, or, in the case of pregnancy, for no crime at all. When a girl becomes pregnant, many families refuse to allow her back home. Institutionalization is often the only available alternative for a young girl, since placement outside public institutions is not as readily available for females as for males. Many foster homes simply refuse to accept female adolescents, especially if they have medical problems (Jolly, 1979, p. 107).

Therefore, in addition to problems common to both sexes, juvenile females have an additional need for medical care related to venereal disease, menstrual complications, and pregnancy-related problems. Juvenile detention and long-term institutions with female populations need to have available health services to meet the special health needs of adolescent girls, and alternative community service programs need to be developed or expanded in order to reduce the institutionalization of females for the purpose of receiving adequate medical attention.

The medical needs of juveniles entering the juvenile justice system become even more significant considering the fact that juveniles are often detained in adult jails. Although it is generally prohibited by federal and state law, a study by the Children's Defense Fund conducted in 1976 found that children are in adult jails in every state they visited. Of the 449 jails visited, 171, or 38.1% held children regularly as a matter of policy. Of those that did not hold children as a matter of general policy, 14.7% acknowledged that they occasionally held children. In addition, they found that unless a juvenile is visibly acutely ill, no medical attention is given. Only 15.8% of the 171 jails holding juveniles provided a medical examination upon admission; 14 jails indicated that trained medical personnel did the examining, and the rest were "eyeball" examinations performed by the custodial staff (Children's Defense Fund, 1976, p. 35).

Considering the poor quality of medical care in jails in general, juveniles with medical problems at admission are unlikely to have their medical needs identified and less likely to have them treated. The findings of the

Children's Defense Fund regarding the lack of medical care in jails are supported by other studies. According to a report on the census of jails in 1972, only one of every eight jails has some sort of in-house medical facility (U.S. Department of Justice, 1975, p. 7). The health needs of juveniles admitted to adult jails frequently are increased due to the high incidence of illness among adult inmates upon admission to jails or during incarceration (see, e.g., American Bar Association, 1974; Goldsmith, 1974).

A recent survey of federal and state prisons and local jails by the General Accounting Office (GAO) also found that "health care delivery systems of most prisons and jails are inadequate, and many correctional agencies are under increasing pressure, particularly from the courts, to provide more adequate levels of care" (Report to the Congress by the Comptroller of the United States, 1978).

An earlier review of adult jail medical care also supports the GAO findings regarding the poor quality of medical care provided inmates. A significant number of health facilities and programs were found to be overutilized, obsolete, unsafe, and therefore unsatisfactory. Although the situation may be improving slowly, generally there remains a barren wasteland of medical care in adult jails in this country (Goldsmith, 1974, p. 575).

Therefore, although there may be some indication of general improvement in medical care, a number of problems remain. In addition to a need for financial resources to improve medical care in facilities and institutions, the problems of staff turnover which decrease the continuity of care, and the clash between medical and penal philosophies, the impact of the correctional environment upon the delivery of quality medical care is one of the biggest problems in penal medical care which impacts on medical services on a day-to-day basis (Protzel, 1972, p. 507).

The medical problem per se (in a juvenile detention institution) is not different as it relates to the diagnosis, treatment, and prognosis of disease. Detention does not alter the course of appendicitis or the healing of a fracture. The restrictions of detention may, of course, alter the juvenile's psychiatric and psychological reactions; removal from the family environment may alter the juvenile's reaction and modify many aspects of the practice of medicine. The situation is likely to include a patient who is anxious, hostile, and prone to exaggerate; a physician who is suspicious regarding the veracity of statements; and security personnel who are reluctant to move the juvenile to an outside source of medical care in case the juvenile is "faking." The medical practitioner dealing with these problems must be an astute diagnostician to discern the serious complaints and pathology from the complaints generated by the sophisticated juvenile who has merely come to sick call for a change of scenery or to attempt to wrangle a pill from the doctor for their own nonmedical use or for trading purposes.

To illustrate the difficulties in delivering medical care in juvenile detention facilities or institutions, it may be useful to contrast it with the practice of medicine as it occurs in private practice. In private practice, the patient freely chooses the physician out of respect for the physician's ability and reputation. In addition, the patient comes to the physician out of desire to get better. The patient tells the physician the truth regarding the illness and accepts the physician's advice and treatment. In correctional institutions, in contrast, the patient (inmate) has no choice of physician, usually has little respect for the ability of the physician, and often tries to manipulate the physician-patient relationship for other than medical reasons. The patient (inmate) therefore often fabricates the symptoms or illness and rejects the physician's advice and treatment. Furthermore, the patient (inmate) is seldom thankful for the physician's assistance, but rather perceives the physician as part of the custodial staff of the institution.

Medical program recommendations advocate that medical care in a correctional institution be carried out by a group or clinic having no administrative connection with the institutional security personnel, that they operate entirely separately from the "jailing" or detention "lockup" aspects, and that they be the responsibility of community medical services or the health department of the state rather than a part of the correctional institution.

Space, equipment, and staffing of the detention unit are essential for the proper practice of medicine and should conform to the standards set up by the AMA Committee on Standards in Juvenile Institutional Facilities.

It is in the rather hostile environment of a security-oriented facility that the medical, nursing, and dental professions must entrench themselves and attempt to gain the confidence and good will of the entering juvenile. It is in spite of this environment that the medical process must of necessity focus upon the detection of medical and dental problems, provide essential treatment, and study and treat these problems with the goal of assisting in the overall rehabilitation of the juvenile.

The following presentation provides a summary of some of the major problems confronting the delivery of medical care to juveniles in a correctional institutional setting.

Medical confidentiality is a basic legal right under the recent Privacy Act. The security staff and the nonmedical rehabilitative staff is, of course, entitled to all information which might further their rehabilitative efforts. However, privileged medical information should be treated as such and should be recorded and filed in an medically confidential manner. Respecting the rights of the detainee will pay dividends in the staff's being the recipient of information that would otherwise not be forthcoming. Release of confidential medical information should almost invariably be only with the consent of the detainee.

The administration and responsibility for medical and dental matters should be vested in a medical director. Unfortunately, the prescriptive package *Health Care in Correctional Institutions* points out the low administrative rank accorded the medical administrative function. This low administrative position within the detention or correctional institution contributes continuing problems and conflicts over penal and medical priorities. Unless medical personnel are given authority in budgetary and administrative matters, mediocrity will prevail in the personnel attracted to or gravitating into positions of importance in correctional medicine. The part-time medical consultant is very desirable, but there must be knowledgeable and authoritative medical administrative guidance with a voice in the medical program destiny within the correctional environment.

Drug overdose, alcohol intoxication, and drug and alcohol habituation will be frequent problems; equipment and adequate trained staff in resuscitation methods will be necessary for coping with the emergency aspects of these clinical situations; the serious cases require prompt transfer to the hospital emergency room staffed with a physician. Infirmary rooms must be available for nursing care and observation for the milder cases and for the convalescent cases returning from the acute care hospital; these will include convalescing medical and surgical cases as well as the psychiatric cases requiring observation and treatment.

Suicide prevention is a most important program in a detention and long-term correctional facility. Smielek and Spitz analyzed 24 deaths in local Wayne County, Michigan jails in 1976 and 1977. Of the 25 deaths, 20 were suicides, with one accident, one homicide, one of natural causes, and two of undetermined causes, possibly drug related. The authors comment:

> The most important finding of this study is that almost all (24 of 25) deaths ocurred within the first 24 hours of incarceration. This is

better understood when one considers the sense of isolation, helplessness, and despair often experienced by new prisoners. The body search, fingerprinting, photographs, and delousing, part of regular jail admission protocol, add to the humiliation and loss of contact with the outside world. Intoxicated prisoners should be recognized as greater suicidal risks . . . Bizarre behavior and speech suggestive of an underlying mental disorder or evidence of past suicide attempts . . . should alert jail personnel to a potential suicide attempt . . . Wayne County, Michigan, has installed video monitors in their holding cells. The equipment and installation cost about $3,000. Its use has resulted in the prevention of 12 suicides to date (Smielek and Spitz, 1978, p. 2564).

Hearing defects remediable by surgery or benefited by hearing aid apparatus may greatly enhance rehabilitative efforts. Consultation with an otolaryngologist and possible referral to a hearing center are indicated for appropriate treatment of these cases.

Juveniles with visual acuity defects remediable by correction with glasses should be furnished with these glasses and encouraged to wear them. Surgical correction of Strabismus (crossed eyes) may not always increase visual acuity in the older child; however, surgical correction of this condition may be indicated for cosmetic reasons if the defect is quite disfiguring. Consultation between a "team" may be of considerable value, such a team consisting of physician, opthalmologist, psychiatrist, and psychologist. Any increase in visual acuity and awareness may greatly increase the learning ability of the child, a great positive factor in the rehabilitation of the young delinquent.

Cosmetic abnormalities may, at times, be a factor in the overall etiology of juvenile delinquency; scars may need revision for cosmetic reasons as well as for functional improvement in some cases. All attempts at cosmetic improvement must be accompanied by a concerted effort of psychotherapy in the overall effort to improve ego image.

The prevalence of tattoos is a problem that is rather unique to the delinquency subculture. The incidence of tattoos on incoming wards in the juvenile justice system is in the realm of 50%. Many of these tattoos are self-inflicted or inserted by peers or fellow gang members. A tattooed gang mark displayed by an individual while in some other gang's "turf" may invite a "stomping" or "rat packing." Thus, in a detention unit, such a tattoo may literally become a matter of life or death! Tattoo removal services should be established. Facial tattoos often will require the service of the plastic surgeon. The "salabrasion" method of tattoo removal in which the tattoo is vigorously rubbed with salt (Manchester, 1974; Crittenden, 1971) is a fairly simple technique which can be learned by a physician through a minimal amount of training and should be acquired by physicians and surgeons providing services to detention units.

Congenital defects and abnormalities require evaluation and efforts made to direct the individual needing such treatment into appropriate channels. Medical social work is necessary to explore socialized services; the congenital heart defect may need referral to a cardiac surgery center; the harelip or cleft palate, no doubt previously repaired in infancy, may need revision by a plastic surgeon trained in maxillo-facial procedures. Again, there is the need for a team approach involving the physician and social worker in exploring possibilities of services and in recommending to administration and the court a course of action.

Locomotor disabilities should be evaluated for possible correction or improvement. Residual traumatic disabilities such as knee cartilage injuries suffered in football or other athletic contests, old tendon injuries from past lacerations, and old fracture sequellae, may greatly limit a potentially active youth; these should be remedied in order to improve chances of rehabilitation and to qualify the individual as a wage earner upon reaching adulthood.

Dyslexia with its vague and imprecise knowledge should be researched further by a team of medical and paramedical specialists. Any possibility of enhancing a youth's learning ability and capability needs thorough exploration. A neurological consultaton should be a routine in these cases, and a neurologist and a visual expert, an ophthalmologist, should be on the evaluation team, along with educational and learning experts.

Society has an obligation to juveniles with crippling functional, medical, or emotional problems. These juveniles have a right to reasonable efforts to have such dysfunctions identified and diagnosed at an early age and to be provided appropriate and adequate treatment.

The least appropriate of the children and youth-service systems to be dealing with this group of children with special problems is the control-oriented, fault-finding, and often stigmatizing juvenile justice system. Unfortunately, the juvenile justice system often becomes involved by default. Therefore, every effort should be expended toward achieving early diagnosis and provision of treatment by the most suitable of the other children-serving systems, most of which are voluntary, noncoercive, and treatment oriented.

The screening, diagnosis, and planning of treatment, as well as the delivery of treatment which is geared to juveniles with special problems, should be available to the juvenile services system. Additionally, screening or identification of special problems should exist at the juvenile court intake level. When a juvenile with an identified special problem is referred to juvenile court intake, the intake worker's orientation should be to divert the juvenile to an appropriate community service agency without court involvement, unless it is clear that the authority and jurisdiction of the court is warranted.

An analysis of the laws supportive of the approach toward meeting the needs of juveniles with special problems indicates that, for the most part, the necessary legislation presently exists.

Therefore, the major need is not for more federal legislation, but for more advocacy efforts to provide for the necessary modifications of the laws and procedures in order to overcome the often overly restrictive eligibility requirements, such as those that require court wardships or the removal of the juvenile from the home. Advocacy efforts can help strengthen the requirements for quality service to juveniles with special problems; encourage increased financial support and proper enforcement and monitoring of treatment programs; as well as foster improved linkage and coordination among programs.

REFERENCES

Brecher, E. M. & Della Penna, R. D. *Health Care in Correctional Institutions.* U.S. Department of Justice, Law Enforcement Assistance Administration, National Institute of Law Enforcement and Criminal Justice. Washington, DC: U.S. Government Printing Office, September 1975.

Carper, J. Medical care of delinquent adolescent boys. *Pediatric Clinics of North America*, May 1974, *20*(2), 209-210.

Children's Defense Fund. *Children in Adult Jails.* Washington, DC, 1976.

Crittenden, F. M. Salabrasion: Removal of tattoos by superficial abrasion with table salt. *CUTIS*, March 1971, *7*.

Goldsmith, S. B. The status of prison health care: A review of the literature. *Public Health Reports*, November/December 1974, *89*(6), 569-575.

Jolly, M. K. Young, female, and outside the law: A call for justice for the girl delinquent. In R. Crow & G. McCarthy (Eds.), *Teenage Women in the Juvenile Justice System: Changing Values.* New Directions for Young Women, Inc., 1979, 107.

Kosidlak, J. G. Improving health care for troubled youths. *American Institute of Nursing*, January 1976 *75(1), 95-97.*

Lewis, D. O. & Shanok, S. S. Medical histories of delinquent and nondelinquent children: An epidemiological study. *American Journal of Psychiatry*, September 1977, *134*, 1010-1025.

Manchester, G. The removal of commercial tattoos by abrasion with table salt. *Plastic and Reconstructive Surgery*, May 1974, *53*(5).

Protzel, M. S. Nursing behind bars. *American Journal of Nursing*, March 1972, *27*(3), 505-508.

Report to the congress by the comptroller of the United States. A federal strategy is needed to help improve medical and dental care in prisons and jails. December 22, 1978.

Ris, H. W. Comprehensive medical care in a state institute for youth in Wisconsin. In R. Bodine & R. Brown (Comps. & Eds.), *Guidelines for Health Care in Juvenile Court Institutions*. American Academy of Pediatrics, Chapter One, Northern California, n.d., 225-231.

Ris, H. W., & Dodge, R. W. Gonorrhea in adolescent girls in a closed population. *American Journal of the Diseases of Children*, 1972, *123*, 206-209.

Smielek, J. E. & Spitz, W. U. Death behind bars. *Journal of the American Medical Association*, December 1978, *23*, 240.

U.S. Department of Justice, Law Enforcement Assistance Administration, National Criminal Justice Information and Statistics Service. *The nation's jails: A report on the census of jails from the 1972 survey of inmates of local jails*. Washington, DC: U.S. Government Printing Office, May 1975.

THE ABUSE OF STATUS OFFENDERS
IN PRIVATE HOSPITALS

Michael Robin

ABSTRACT. On the basis of 3 years of experience as a psychiatric assistant in a Twin Cities hospital, the author argues that placement in a psychiatric ward is essentially abusive to status offenders. He points out that many of these young people have been abused, but that they are treated on the ward not as abused children, but as problem children. Being locked up, having to follow treatment plans, being threatened with isolation and medication, and being treated by insecure staff with insufficient training are all, this author argues, abusive.

Because the Juvenile Justice and Delinquency Prevention Act of 1974 placed restrictions on the use of public facilities for the treatment of status offenders, many states are now placing status offenders in private psychiatric hospitals, circumventing the deinstitutionalization law. Unfortunately, we have no national statistics on the extent of hospitalizations of status offenders, and if we did, they would likely be gross underestimates, as most status offenders are not admitted to hospitals under a court order but under the threat of one, usually by a parent or social worker.

As a matter of definition, status offenses are those noncriminal behaviors such as incorrigibility, running away, and truancy that are considered illegal because of a child's age. Status offenders are by definition "out-of-control," and treatment in the hospitals tends to focus on modifying or changing those behaviors that are deemed unacceptable to adult society. The problem is that by focusing on behavior as such, and by defining children as out-of-control, the complex reasons why childen act out are missed. Definition is crucial; for as Mark Twain said, "If the only tool you have is a hammer, then you tend to treat every problem as if it were a nail." How children's problems are defined will have major implications for the course and content of their treatment and is at the root of what I

Michael Robin is staff researcher with the Minnesota Supreme Court Juvenile Justice Study Commission, 114 TNA, 122 Pleasant Street, University of Minnesota, Minneapolis, MN 55455. Requests for reprints should be addressed to Michael Robin at that address.

see as the considerable emotional and physical abuse that adolescent patients endure in psychiatric hospitals.

This paper is based on my 3 years of experience as a psychiatric assistant in a Twin Cities hospital. I will try to stay away from horror stories of gross abuse, for that is not my point. Rather I intend to show how the system itself, when working properly, is abusive to children. My initial reaction to this program was quite positive. I was caught up, like many others, in the power I had over children. However, as I gained more experience and my knowledge of child development increased through my education, I came to reject the system.

Status Offenses and Child Abuse

Status offenders are often children who have been abused, yet in this hospital they are treated as offenders. Only occasionally is a child placed on the unit with a specific clinical disorder such as schizophrenia, depression, or anorexia nervosa; instead, most patients are diagnosed as having behavior or conduct disorders, like status offenses. A number of investigators have pointed out that many children in institutions have suffered earlier abuse and neglect within their own families, foster families, or other institutions. Douglas Kline, an educator at Utah State University, testified before Congress in 1979 that "the children who come into conflict with the law and ultimately populate our institutions are for the most part victims of physical abuse, neglect, abandonment, and/or sexual molestation *before* they came into conflict with juvenile authorities and *before* they are committed to institutional environments." The New York Select Committee on Child Abuse found in a 1978 study that nearly 50% of the families who had been reported for child abuse and neglect eventually had at least one child taken to court for delinquency and ungovernability. The summary of the report cautioned, however, that child maltreatment cannot be used as an indicator or predicator of future juvenile misbehavior. The two are strongly associated, but other factors affect whether or not a child becomes delinquent or ungovernable.

Such facts are consistent with my own experience as a psychiatric assistant. Many of the patients had indeed suffered abuse, both physical and sexual, or had been neglected. While most staff knew that the children had suffered serious maltreatment, they generally believed that these children's behavior had elicited abuse, rather than that the behavior disturbances were symptoms of abuse and neglect. As in most child care institutions, the psychiatric staff were largely untrained and ignorant of the special needs of abused children, and they frequently responded to the children in a manner similar to that of the children's abusive parents.

Dynamics of Child Abuse and Neglect

The major psychological dynamic in abused children is identification with their aggressors (Martin & Rodeheffer, 1980). That is, children respond to their maltreatment by assuming their own "badness"; for why would their parents, who are so wonderful, abuse them unless they were bad? Abused children typically have great difficulty directing their rage toward their aggressors, for they assume that if they did, their parents or caretakers would go away. Consequently, they develop what might be called a shame-based personality (Bach, 1980). They are bad; they are responsible for the abuse, as they deserve the abuse that comes to them. In fact, abused children are particularly adept in provoking punishment or rejection from others, for when they get it, it confirms who they are, that they are indeed shameful and unworthy.

Abused children learn to survive by accommodating their needs to the needs of the aggressors within their environments. They have a hypervigilant attitude, constantly fearful of assault or invasion, with little ability to take for granted the care and nurture of their caregivers. They become "watchers," acutely aware of mood changes in the adults around them, and they develop a rather "chameleon nature," learning to shift their behavior according to what is expected of them and denying their own impulses. The children learn to avoid punishment by becoming experts at "passive resistance," by feigning acceptance of what others demand. On the surface, then, abused children try to control and manipulate everyone and everything; however, this behavior is less willful than assumed and is based on fear of rejection or punishment.

Additionally, abused children are valued most when they are meeting the needs and expectations of their parents. This is especially apparent when children are obeying or simply staying out of their parents' way. They are not valued in their own right for their own needs, values, and interests. Furthermore, their efforts at being competent or independent frequently result in verbal or physical abuse. Abused children are thus more apt to feel that they lack control over their environments and that external factors, rather than their own efforts, determine the outcome of events. Abused children are essentially joyless, lonely creatures who have a poor sense of themselves, lack initiative and confidence, and find relationships with others quite stressful.

The process whereby children learn self-control is also disrupted in abusive families. They identify with a parent who is a model of aggressive behavior but who denies expressions of aggression from the children. The children, lacking effective self-control, alternate between extreme inhibition and sudden volatile outbursts. Their lack of self-control is also seen in their tendency to lie and steal when not monitored. Their efforts, through misbehavior, at establishing a separate identity and independence from their parents tend to be more symbolic than real. Acting out serves to deny children's dependency needs and repeats the earlier traumatic experiences of punishment, abandonment, or ridicule. Misbehaving then becomes a means to control the environment and make it predictable, but it covers up the underlying shame and fear of not being loved.

Daily Regimen

Many child-rearing practices that would be considered abusive if done in the family are legally and socially condoned by our society in the name of discipline and treatment. It is in the normal course of treatment that many children are abused. When children enter the hospital, they are quickly oriented to its rules and regimen, and great effort is made to establish the authority of the staff over the children. The locked door is the most obvious and salient symbol of the children's powerlessness in their new environment. The children are not allowed to be outside the unit until the staff considers them trustworthy enough not to run away and until they are working on their treatment goals, which routinely takes 2 to 3 weeks and sometimes longer. Thus, to maintain control within the institution, an artificially restricted environment is set up, so that children are forced to comply with authority to regain the privileges they have hitherto taken for granted. Many children report feelings of shame and humiliation at being locked up and resent the implication that they are somehow dangerous or crazy. Incest victims and other victims of abuse are routinely placed on this unit, along with children who have committed serious crimes; this tends to reinforce their idea that they are bad and they have done something wrong. The problem is that this hospital makes no distinction between those patients who need and those who do not need to be locked up, so that many who do not need to be locked up suffer the consequences of inappropriate placement.

The daily regimen is designed primarily for the convenience of the staff in maintaining control over the children and has little to do with the developmental needs of the individual child. The design of the unit allows for constant observation, so that the only opportunity children have to be unmonitored is when they are in their own rooms, and even here privacy is violated by frequent room checks. Moreover, the staff can, at will, search children's rooms or persons, further violating their personal and bodily integrity. This is clearly not a relaxed, secure atmosphere free from constant scrutiny, something Konpka considers vital to healthy group life in residential treatment (1972, p. 172). The tension is enhanced further because the unit has no gym or outdoor play area. Many children, lacking an outlet for their pent-up energy and emotions, respond by chain smoking, overeating, general irritability, or occasional violent outbursts. Very few staff appreciate how the environment of the institution itself—its restrictions, its boredom, its close living quarters—may encourage children to act out. In their view, the children's behavior is the problem.

Hospitalized children are expected to follow a plethora of depersonalized rules and regulations which teach them compliance more than they teach them responsible behavior. In many messages given by the staff, explicit communications, for instance that children should be responsible for themselves, are contradicted by implicit ones. Children on the ward are never allowed to decide for themselves what they wish to do and to do it unmonitored. They are given care plans with a variety of target behaviors that are part of their treatment plan. In most cases, the children do not understand the language or the purpose of the care plan, nor are they consulted on its content. Nonetheless, they are expected to use it and receive feedback each hour on how well they are fulfilling their behavioral goals. Bettleheim and Sylvester have argued that compliance with stereotyped rules may constitute adequate adjustment to the institution but allows the child little opportunity for spontaneity and responsible decision making. "Complete determination by external rules prevents the development of inner controls. Emotional conflicts cannot be utilized toward personality growth because they are not intrapsychic conflicts, but only occasional clashes between instinctive tendencies and impersonal external rules" (1972, p. 71).

Children are always expected to accept the feedback given them by the staff, which tends to be negative and critical. Many disturbed children become easily discouraged by negative criticism, as it affirms their already low self-concept. Generally, the staff does not understand the importance of positive reinforcement as a more effective influence on behavioral change. All too often, staff are insensitive to the children's intellectual and developmental level and use abstract, complicated language or speak in a harsh degrading tone. Children are not allowed to disagree with staff, and because accepting feedback is tied to earning privileges, most children learn that it is not worthwhile to argue with staff. In addition, they are not encouraged to think for themselves and to learn how to evaluate what they hear about themselves, to decide what sounds plausible and what does not. In effect, what the children really learn is to manipulate adults by giving them the compliance they demand. In this role reversal, the needs and views of the children are discounted by the adults around them.

In the ward, children are denied the right to decide whom they will trust and in whom they will confide or even if they will trust anyone at all. For example, each day children have a "one-to-one" where they talk over their problems with a staff member. Because the staff person changes frequently, children are actively discouraged from talking with only a few people and are expected to talk openly with any staff member. Should they refuse to talk with someone, they might be punished for allegedly not working on their problems. Because talking about their problems is tied to earning privileges, many children survive by learning how to speak about themselves with psychological terms that they do not understand. As Piaget points out, adolescents are capable of abstract thought, of reflecting on their own behavior and motives; but the development of abstract thought depends on the maturational level of the child, not only on the chronological (1975). To expect children who have been abused or who have learning difficulties to verbalize their feelings is abusive in itself, for it expects more than the behavior of which the children are capable. Furthermore, by discouraging primary relationships, the hospital is denying the children what they need most, a consistent caretaker who offers unconditional nurturance. The ever changing caretaker is, according to Rutter, one of the great failures of institutions in providing therapeutic intervention, for it continues and reinforces the lack of consistent care from which abused children have already suffered (Rutter, 1979, pp. 147-154).

Discipline and Punishment

Discipline in the psychiatric ward relies heavily on isolation and seclusion. For rule violations or for not working satisfactorily on their treatment goals, children are routinely placed on room restriction. As a matter of course, when children are placed in their rooms, the rooms are stripped of all personal or leisure items such as books, games, or radios. The length of time children are kept in seclusion varies from a short period for minor infractions to 24-hour periods or longer for more serious violations. For example, if staff judge that a particular child is not working hard enough on resolving problems, that child will be placed on room restriction until his or her attitude changes, which in some cases has been up to a week or more. In one extreme case, a 13-year-old hyperactive boy was kept on room restriction for 6 weeks, until he acknowledged the pain of his family situation. During this time, this child was not allowed any communication with his family or his fellow patients, nor was he allowed any recreational activities or to go to school. This practice is torture, the principle of which is that with sufficient pain, people will change their behavior.

The "time-out" room is a small, bare room of concrete walls and screened windows, used when children are out of control. It can also be used when room seclusion has not produced the desired behavior change. Seclusion in the time-out room tends to produce initial affective responses of rage and terror, then helplessness, and eventually resignation and compliance. Wadeson has suggested that seclusion may encourage paranoid reactions in disturbed patients (1980, pp. 163-170). They fear being overpowered, "looked at," and controlled. Expressions of bitterness and humiliation are frequently reported weeks and months after the isolation incident. Furthermore, many abused and disturbed children harbor deep anxiety about being abandoned, unwanted, and unloved, which tends to be reinforced by their time-out room experiences. Miller, drawing on the work of D. Winnicott, argues that anxious adolescents, like infants, need to be able to project their anxiety onto their care givers, who then absorb it and return back to the children a sense of security (1978, pp. 434-447). Holding out-of-control children rather than isolating them can give anxious adolescents the equivalent of the cuddling mothers give their infants. Emotional development occurs when children are allowed to express their feelings without the fear of punishment or abandonment. This institution, instead of hiring adequate numbers of skilled staff, resorts to isolation or to drugs like Thorazine or Haldol for the management of disruptive behavior, which is another example of abuse.

Needs of Staff

The attitude of the staff toward these children is markedly ambivalent; they claim to be nurturant and child centered, but they are also hostile and demand disciplined and controlled behavior. The concern for order and obedience leads to denial of the children's needs and often to abuse. The techniques of control and the forms of communication that staff use with patients are generally not those they would use with their own children. These children are said to be "different," to suffer primarily from a lack of consistent limit setting rather than from a lack of love. Miller notes that the shaming, disparaging, and controlling seem to have a "particularly disruptive and sadistic element to them" (1978, p. 440), one that tends to assume an exaggerated willfulness on the part of the misbehaving child. These inappropriate techniques may arise because the staff are inadequately trained and supervised for the work they do. They lack an appreciation and understanding of the behavioral dynamics of child abuse, so they often overreact to the children's oppositional behavior. Such instances tend to heighten the staff's sense of helplessness and lack of control over the children. Staff will thus act to restore their authority, and, in the process, they often disregard the meaning of the children's behavior. Staff need children to be compliant, as it gives them a sense of power that is otherwise lacking in their lives. They tend to exaggerate their own importance in the children's lives, and they do not appreciate the effect of their own feelings and insecurities on the therapeutic relationship. Staff powerlessness is reinforced by their status within the hospital structure, where they receive low pay, have little room for advancement, and are expected to be compliant within the hierarchical structure defined by the medical model of treatment. The staff are unable to direct their frustrations within the system, so they turn to the child for a sense of power. Just as the staff have little understanding of how their own work environment may affect their feelings, they are unappreciative of how they stifle the initiative and autonomy of children by imposing too many restrictions on their behavior.

Conclusion

Abused children have a remarkable ability to provoke further punishment and mistreatment from their caretakers. In this study, I have attempted to show that by defining delinquent children as ungovernable rather than as abused, hospital psychiatric wards reinforce character traits that are rooted in earlier abuse. More than limits and discipline, what abused children need are consistent care and nurture, or simply love. As Ashley Montagu wrote, "no child adequately loved ever became a delinquent or murderer" (1971, p. 174). If we are to provide treatment to delinquent children, we need to reject their efforts to push us away or provoke us to punish them. We need to offer more than rules and regimentation, for they need more than simply to be controlled. We need to provide environments that are safe and predictable, but most of all loving.

REFERENCES

Bach, J. *An ideological framework for understanding the emotional layers of the shame-based personality*. Unpublished paper, 1980.

Bettleheim, B., & Sylvester, E. A therapeutic milieu. In J. Whittaker & A. Treschman (Eds.), *Children away from home*. Chicago: Aldine Publishing Company, 1972.

Kline, D. Testimony before subcommittee on child and human development, January 24, 1979.

Konopka, G. The role of the group in residential treatment. In J. Whittaker & A. Treschman (Eds.), *Children away from home*. Chicago: Aldine Publishing Company, 1972.

Martin, H. & Rodeheffer, M. The psychological impact of abuse on children. In G. Williams & J. Money, *Traumatic abuse and neglect of children at home*. Baltimore: John Hopkins Press, 1980, pp. 254-62.

Miller, D. Early adolescence: Its psychology, psychopathalogy, and implications for therapy. In S. Feinstein & P. Giovacchini (Eds.), *Adolescent psychiatry*, Vol. VI. 1978, pp. 434-447.

Montagu, A. *Touching: The human significance of the skin*. Columbia University Press, 1971.

Piaget, J. Intellectual development of the adolescent. In A. H. Esman (Ed.), *The psychology of adolescence*. New York: International Universities Press, 1975.

Rutter, M. Separation experiences. Journal of Pediatrics, July 1979, 95(1), 147-154.

Summary report of the relationship between child abuse and neglect and later socially deviant behavior. New York Select Committee on Child Abuse, March 1978.

Wadison, H. *Art psychotherapy*. New York: Wiley Press, 1980, 163-170.

CHILDREN'S RIGHTS ON ENTERING
THERAPEUTIC INSTITUTIONS

Derek Miller
Robert A. Burt

ABSTRACT. The authors argue from a consideration of psychological development that adolescents are not always able to make decisions about whether or not they need treatment. They say that the courts should make sure that adolescents receive adequate treatment instead of making sure they consent to treatment.

Laws regulating access for adolescents to residential psychiatric facilities are being reexamined. The existing law has provided two paths into such institutions: placement by the parents or placement by the juvenile court. Both routes give the adolescent no legally sanctioned voice.

New rules being offered stipulate that adolescents who protest their hospitalization may obtain court review and representation by appointed attorneys. The idea is also presented that, apart from cases in which the adolescent is being wayward, courts may take custody of an adolescent only by adult standards, i.e., when he or she has been adjudged dangerous to self or others.

Critiques of the current law point to the manifest inadequacies of residential facilities for children and adolescents, particularly those under the aegis of the juvenile court. In effect, these critiques also involve psychiatric hospitals for children. They somtimes appear to reject any therapeutic possibility in any psychiatric facility without the explicit consent of the adolescent; thus they rest on a fundamental misconception of adolescent psychology.

The purpose of this paper is to delineate those aspects of adolescent

Derek Miller is Professor of Psychiatry and Director of the Adolescent Program, Northwestern Memorial Hospitals, 259 East Erie, Chicago, IL 60611. Robert A. Burt is Professor of Law, Yale University, New Haven, CT 06520. The article is reprinted, with an introduction by Derek Milller, from *The American Journal of Psychiatry*, Vol. 134:2, pp. 153-156, February 1977. Copyright 1977, the American Psychiatric Association. Reprinted by permission. Requests for reprints should be addressed to Derek Miller at the above address.

psychological development which must be considered in any decision regarding psychiatric residential placement. We will review the issue of consent in the context of developmental psychology and identify a role for court supervision of adolescent psychiatric placements that does not work at odds with the psychological needs of adolescents.

Techniques of Adolescent Communication

The communication techniques of adolescents may differ from those of adults. Depending on their maturational age, adolescents may be highly concrete in their thinking (Flavell, 1963) and may have little or no affective awareness that their present actions influence the future.

As a communication device, words, which are least meaningful in infancy and most meaningful in adulthood, may be considerably less important for the adolescent than action. Concrete thinking is related to physiological and psychological development, as well as to social class and educational attainment. It implies a limited capacity for future orientation, which is related to the development of abstract thought.

The important communication techniques of adolescents are behavioral, i.e., (1) acting out (impulsive relief of internal tension or externalization of internal conflict by the conscious or unconscious manipulation of external reality); (2) acting up (socially unacceptable behavior apparently designed to test the adult capacity for care and control; some types of delinquent behavior may fall into this group); and (3) playacting (experimental behavior designed to gain personal experience of the environment and to test oneself; initially, sexual activity may involve playacting).

These communication techniques may become developmental stumbling blocks if they are inappropriately gratifying. Words themselves may be an action communication. Adolescents struggling for autonomy may deny any need for adult assistance. Thus they act out independent wishes, act up to test the strength of the external world, and playact the experience of defiance.

Legal Changes and Parent Authority

Legislatures and courts have not substantially attempted to improve the inadequacies of facilities for disturbed and disturbing adolescents. However, these bodies have chosen to intervene most dramatically in parent-child relationships in the provison of psychiatric treatment (Ellis, 1974, pp. 840-916). The Supreme Court considered a case in which a lower court held that every child placed by his or her parents in a residential psychiatric institution has a right to an appointed attorney (*Bartley* v. *Kremens*, 1974, pp. 1039-1058; Supreme Court review granted, 1976, p. 3525). One state court provided that adolescents may themselves decide to leave treatment at the age of 16 unless they are committable under adult standards (*Melville* v. *Sabbatino*, 1973). Another state legislature provided that adolescents at least 13 years old may invoke court hearings to protest their parents' placement decisions and that treatment personnel must initiate "therapeutic" contact with the adolescents by "warning" them of these rights (Michigan Mental Health Code, 1974, p. 1417).

These rules disregard central issues of adolescent psychology. In adolescence there is inevitably a covert and often an overt conflict between parents and child, if only because the child is struggling for autonomy. Laws that automatically give unexamined authority to parents to make a wide range of decisions on behalf of their children support family units, which are historically part of a stable network of human relationships. To some extent, the law reinforces a preexisting sense of value that adolescents accord to parents, even though conflicts might exist.

The more children are isolated from stable social networks, the greater is the stress on their relationship with their parents (Miller, 1974).

The nuclear family has been weakened by its increasing isolation due to horizontal and social mobility and by the general instability of society. By introducing formal adversarial techniques into parent-child relationships, recent changes in the law reinforce the likelihood of the disintegration of the nuclear family.

In many states adolescents may obtain treatment for venereal disease or drug abuse without the knowledge or consent of their parents (Raitt, 1974, pp. 1417-1456). There is clinical psychiatric evidence that when authority figures implicitly or explicitly act with children against their parents, the results of treatment are generally unsatisfactory. If the law reinforces the pseudo-autonomy rather than the real autonomy of adolescents, by implying that parental intervention is unsatisfactory, it is likely that results will be equally disappointing.

By acting on the belief that truth can be arrived at by adversarial techniques, the proposed changes in the law miss such ambiguous issues as unconscious parental collusion in and provocation of disturbed behavior in adolescents (Miller, 1974, pp. 522-524). The problem in the psychological treatment of disturbed adolescents often appears to be the reluctance of parents to support therapeutic endeavors, not their overanxiety to dump their youngsters on the mental health system.

For a number of reasons, the result of the proposed changes in the law is likely to be that adolescents who could be treated effectively in inpatient psychiatric facilities may not get treatment anywhere. It is almost inevitable that psychologically disturbed adolescents who are struggling for autonomy will defy authority by verbally denying that they need help. The more narcissistic the adolescent, the more intense is the struggle. Such youngsters often have parents who are unable to withstand this type of pressures, as the following case report illustrates.

Case 1. A 15-year-old boy was referred to a psychiatrist because his parents had heard him on the telephone discussing drug abuse. When interviewed, he revealed that he was using street drugs moderately but that he was a very active dealer, athough he was only a middleman.

He talked of his drug dealing with affective coldness and indicated that his goal was to make as much money as possible. He said that if his father attempted to interfere with him, he would have to use physical force against him. When he was asked about this, he indicated that he kept a knife and a gun at home and carried one of them to school every day to protect himself from possible attack by other students. He had never been in a situation in which he needed to defend himself, but he said that if he were attacked he would use his weapon.

This potentially treatable young man was a candidate for admission to a hospital in a state whose law invited judicial review of adolescent admissions. He refused to be admitted without a court order. His parents felt that they could not risk having the judge refuse to have their son admitted because they would then be fearful of their lives. Nothing was done.

Legal Changes and Residential Care

Many psychiatric residential institutions refuse to consider admitting young people who are likely to be involved with the courts. The institutions reason that the treatment of disturbed adolescents is sufficiently difficult without the complication of attorneys, who are easily seduced by adolescents and who appear competitive with physicians (often because of the automatic application of an adversary relationship). Physicians may recognize their own defensiveness with attorneys and prefer not to be involved with them.

The new laws may work antitherapeutically by requiring explicit acquiescence to hospitalization from adolescents who may not have insisted on court proceedings. The psychologically disturbed young person is not permitted to safeguard his or her fragile sense of autonomy by withholding explicit concurrence to hospitalization.

The new rules ignore the potentially disheartening impact on an adolescent of an explicit choice for or against hospitalization. The choice itself may breed feelings of rejection. One boy said to his therapist, "I know what you and Dr. T. and all of the ward staff mean when you tell me over and over again about my rights, and that I can go to court if I don't want to stay, and all that. What you really mean is that you don't want me."

Most adolescents need to feel that they have some choice, even if they really do not. Explicit court commitment of an adolescent is a demand for submission that, even in good treatment setting, is likely to lead to over-compliance, emotional withdrawal, institutional paranoia, and on occasion, planned elopement. Furthermore, when an adolescent in a residential institution calls on the court in an attempt to leave and his or her psychiatrist successfully argues that treatment should continue, the patient may feel that the therapist is being intolerably seductive. The following case report presents an example of this situation.

Case 2. A 16-year-old boy in a psychiatric hospital demanded a court hearing, insisting that he should be released. A strong case was made by his psychiatrist for his retention in a hospital because of suicidal wishes. The court concurred.

The immediate response of the boy was that now he was in the hospital because the psychiatrist wanted him there. He began to lie by omission to his therapist (previously he had been quite honest and direct). He planned to run away and within a week did so quite skillfully. On his return he told his therapist that he had been planning to leave for a week before he actually went. He also said that he was no longer going to talk to his psychiatrist or to the staff. Eventually his passive withdrawal convinced his parents that he should not be in the hospital. His attitude toward the psychiatrist was, "You forced me to be here, now do what you want with me." Treatment foundered.

On the other hand, if the court decides that a youngster should not stay in residential care and recommends out-patient treatment, the psychiatrist who previously treated the youngster is no longer able to do so satisfactorily because he or she is now perceived as devalued.

The important test of psychological well-being is the typical response to stress of the individual concerned. One typical response to stress that occurs in a hospital setting is the demand to be discharged. Direct and explicit confrontation with this demand, coupled with the legal imprimatur of an adversary relationship, may interfere dramatically with the possibility of a successful resolution of the issues surrounding autonomy.

The ultimate goal of psychiatric hospitalization for adolescents is to provide them with opportunities for unlocking their potential for constructive, successful confrontation with the adult world. This is the goal, not the precursor, of therapeutic endeavors.

A Proper Role for the Courts

Individual court hearings to review the cases of adolescents placed in psychiatric facilities by their parents are not the best way to accomplish the goal of ensuring that abuse does not take place. However, the courts have a useful role. In *O'Connor* v. *Donaldson* (1975), the Supreme Court inconclusively addressed the proposition that involuntarily committed adults have a constitutional right to treatment in psychiatric facilities. Lower courts have established wide-ranging standards to define and guarantee the content of treatment rights for involuntarily confined adults. More recently this has been extended to facilities for adolescents and younger children (Burt, 1976, pp. 417-436).

Courts have so far restricted their remedies to the cases of children explicitly committed in court proceedings (Burt, 1976, pp. 417-436; Wyatt, 1972). Most children who are in psychiatric facilities because of their parents' decisions are placed without regard to their stated wishes and are therefore involuntarily placed. Insofar as parental placement power is sanctioned by law, the child's involuntary placement is achieved under state authority.

Legal reformers argue from these two propositions that a court hearing must precede every such placement as a matter of constitutional law. However, this reasoning is not compelling because there are competing constitutional norms. The constitutionally sanctioned idea that personal liberty cannot be deprived without due process of law points toward mandating court hearings on each individual case. However, the constitutional norm that parents have authority to make important child-rearing decisions without state interference points in a different direction (*Wisconsin* v. *Yoder*, 1972; Burt, 1974, pp. 118-143).

The competing values expressed in these constitutionally sanctioned propositions cannot be accommodated through the psychologically false idea that children are always victimized by their parents' placement decisions or through its opposite—that they are never victimized by them. Courts can accommodate both competing values by viewing children placed in psychiatric facilities as voluntary patients for one purpose—that individualized hearings need not precede placement—but as involuntary patients for a different purpose—to permit courts to guarantee the right to treatment for children in any therapeutic residential facility.

A balance should be struck between the competing constitutional norms of maximal personal liberty and parental child-rearing discretion. Courts should scrutinize with special care the degree to which psychiatric residential placement interferes with the child's personal liberty, especially in the use of locked wards, "quiet rooms," physical and chemical restraints, and the restriction of contact with the extrahospital community necessarily involved in geographically remote placement.

There are many opportunities in a psychiatric facility located within a community for contact by its residents with the world outside. Token confinement within physical facilities safeguards the adolescent's right to personal liberty.

For most psychiatrically disturbed young people, the implicit opportunity to run away from a facility, without the pressure of an explicit commitment to stay, provides a reasonably accurate gauge of the patient's essential evaluation of his or her placement. Implicit opportunities for elopement avoid the therapeutic trap (set by individual court hearings) of forcing an explicit acquiescence or protest in response to hospitalization.

Adolescents demonstrate their willingness in action. In typical cases, at least before the promulgation of the new legal rules, they enter the hospital with only token resistance or with no trouble. Elopement from the hospital is a multidetermined communication, but it is relatively rare for young people not to arrange to be caught. Often they return voluntarily.

When an adolescent runs away from an institution and does not return spontaneously, therapeutic personnel should review the individual's entire treatment process. If such flight occurs in a substantial number of cases, such external review agencies as peer review mechanisms overseen by the judiciary are indicated.

Placement in facilities with a capacity for effective security should be reserved for adolescents who would act in ways that are seriously dangerous to themselves or others if they were free in the community. Placement in such facilities should be restricted to those for whom social control is found appropriate in a juvenile court hearing.

The visible security aspects of such placement have critically important therapeutic implications. In secure facilities the adolescent is forced to sacrifice many autonomy values and therefore can easily regress. On the other hand, the court hearing gives high visibility to the proposition that society has found it appropriate to interfere with the autonomy of the particular adolescent. This proposition can assist skilled therapists to confront the youngster with the implications of his or her problem behavior.

This stark confrontation is appropriate for seriously disturbed adolescents who gain so much instinctual gratification from their antisocial behavior that they cannot easily abandon it. It may unnecessarily complicate therapeutic possibilities for most adolescents, however.

To assume that all residential psychiatric facilities for adolescents are equally confining jettisons the possibility of therapeutic work for many adolescents. Laws regulating access of adolescents to psychiatric residential facilities should differ according to the critical differences in degree of security among facilities.

The Quality of Residential Care and Legal Intervention

The severity of the problem presentation in an adolescent does not necessarily relate to the severity of the underlying illness. However, the psychosocial feedback produced by an adolescent's problems can secondarily reinforce personality disturbance. Adolescent problems present most often as disturbances of behavior. Symptoms become intractable when youngsters receive so much instinctual gratification from their problem behavior that they cannot abandon it. It may, for example, be so satisfying to smoke marijuana that there is no reason to do anything else. Adolescents may not be able to give up tormenting their parents for similar reasons. The emotional gratification from the reinforcement of greed associated with successful theft or from the omnipotence associated with suicidal threats may offer similar satisfactions.

Dealing with an actual or potential experience of helplessness is a central issue for the psychologically disturbed adolescent. In all people, a pervasive sense of helplessness carries with it the perception that the world is tormenting and persecutory. The attempts of authority figures to behave in helpful ways, then, is usually felt as coercive. Normative attempts to be benign may produce a startling persecutory response in the youngster; this is especially true in early adolescents and in all members of this age group who are psychologically disturbed.

Disturbed adolescents have some capacity to appraise reality but may have a confused feeling that the world is not as persecutory as they sense it to be. Such adolescents may then manipulate the environment to make individuals within it actually persecutory. Thus, physical restraints, isolation, and behavior modification techniques are used to control adolescent behavior. Disturbed adolescents then begin to feel that they know where they are from such adult responses; to make others persecute them gives them a bizarre sense of mastery. These issues pervade residential care.

The law in some states has not done more than put constraints on such techniques of treatment, but by doing so they may also implicitly be giving such techniques an acceptable imprimatur, a questionable thing to do. The implicit message of such interventions is not generally one which implies the individualized meeting of the needs of disturbed young people.

The indications for hospital care in disturbed adolescents are as follows:

1. Symptomatic behavior that is dangerous to the self or others and/or self-destructive responses to perceived frustration which cannot be contained within interpersonal relationships, with or without appropriate psychopharmacology.

2. Developmentally destructive behavior that similarly cannot be contained. This includes chronic drug abuse, alcoholism, and sexual promiscuity.

3. Psychic pain or great intensity of symptomatic attempts at pain resolution, so that it is impossible for an adolescent to function in an age-appropriate way. This pain cannot be attenuated by out-patient therapeutic intervention with the patient or the family.

4. A psycho-noxious environment that makes the patient inaccessible to therapuetic intervention.

The concept of the "least restrictive alternative" automatically applied cannot treat the specific diagnosable difficulties of adolescents and negates the concept of adequate diagnosis and treatment. Whether or not a child should be in therapeutic hospital care depends on adequate diagnosis as to the etiology of difficulties—the severity of symptoms and how containable they might be.

Most seriously disturbed adolescents end up in residential care, either a hospital or more usually a correctional center. Many of these social systems are psychologically depriving. Institutionalization, which can be defined as an "emotional deficiency disease" or as teaching inmates to lead an "aberrant social life," is common in correctional settings, just as it is in treatment settings starved of resources. Often residential environments become a justification for staff-patient noncommunication and mutual passivity. Nonspecific care, which reinforces emotional and physical growth, is the most difficult to provide in all treatment settings. For example, institutions have to be persuaded that adolescents need to snack in the evening, and in some centers snacking is withdrawn as a punishment. Funding to involve young people in significant creative and imaginative pursuits is rarely present in psychiatric facilities, almost nonexistent in correctional settings.

It is a fantasy to assume that legal intervention automatically corrects these difficulties. If a "right to treatment" suit is instituted, more often than not facilities are closed. If the law intervenes in terms of advocacy in hospitals, the patient is likely to make the advocate temporarily good but then reacts negatively to the disappointment that merely removing the individual from the institution might create. There is no evidence at the present time that significant legal intervention to improve the correctional care of adolescents is taking place.

In the planning of treatment, the generalized developmental needs of young people are not often considered. There is no evidence that legal intervention has assisted this process; neither is there evidence that it has assisted in the provision of more skilled specific care. The adequate treatment of psychologically disturbed adolescents is rarely provided by society, and reinforcing the adversary relationship between parent and child does not improve the situation. Legal intervention also tends to alienate many physicians from the care of children and adolescents. There is a precipitous decline in the number of professionals who are ready to involve themselves in the care of seriously disturbed young people. One reason for this is an unwillingness to enter into an adverse relationship with attorneys whose training in this area sometimes makes them unempathic to the true needs of their young clients.

REFERENCES

Bartley v. *Kremens*, 402 Fed. Supp. 1039-1058 (1975).

Burt, R. A. Developing constitutional rights of, in, and for children. *Law and Contemporary Problems*, 1975, *39*, 118-143.

Burt, R. A. Beyond the right to habilitation. In M. Kindred et al. (Eds.), *The mentally retarded citizen and the law*. New York: Free Press, 1975, 417-436.

Ellis, J. W. Volunteering children: Parental commitment of minors to mental institutions. *California Law Review*, 1974, *62*, 840-916.

Flavell, J. (Ed.). *The developmental psychology of Jean Piaget*. New York: Van Nostrand Reinhold, 1963.

Melville v. *Sabbatino*, 30 Conn. Supp. 320 (Conn 1973).

Michigan Mental Health Code, section 330, 1417 (1974).

Miller, D. *Adolescence: Psychology, psychopathology and psychotherapy*. New York: Jason Aronson, 1974.

O'Connor v. *Donaldson*, 43 US.W 4929 (1975).

Raitt, G. E. The minor's right to consent to medical treatment. *Southern California Law Review*, 1975, *48*, 1417-1456.

Supreme Court review granted. *U.S. Law Week*, 1976, *44*, 3525.

Wisconsin v. *Yoder*, 406 US Rep. (1972).

Wyatt v. *Stickney*, 344 Fed. Supp. 387 (MD Ala 1972).

CHILDREN BEYOND REACH?

Ernest Hirschbach

ABSTRACT. The author argues that some institutional abuse is caused by frustrated attempts to treat children who are not treatable. We could do better, he says, to admit the existence of such children and to adapt some minimal care facilities for housing them.

In *David Copperfield*, Charles Dickens gives an early, immortal description of child abuse in a boys' boarding school. Vividly, he describes the enjoyment that the headmaster, Mr. Creakle, derives from caning his pupils.

> I should think there never can have been a man who enjoyed his profession more than Mr. Creakle did. He had a delight in cutting at the boys, which was like the satisfaction of a craving appetite. I am confident that he couldn't resist a chubby boy, especially; that there was a fascination in such a subject, which made him restless in his mind, until he had scored and marked him for the day. I was chubby myself, and ought to know.

That is a classic description of a sadist who abuses the power of his position to satisfy his urges.

I do not believe there are many Creakles in the children's institutions of today. It is not sadism that produces abuse and violence in our residential settings; more commonly it is frustration, the inability of care providers to handle their deep anger at youngsters who remain elusive and defiant, who "get away with murder."

We are certain that there would be far fewer damaging abuse episodes in residential settings for children if child care workers only realized that

Ernest Hirschbach is Director Emeritus, Summerhill Homes, Montreal, Quebec. Acknowledgement is made to Mrs. Elana Kruger, Gert Morgensteen, MD, and Jim and Susan Upham, who made corrections. Requests for reprints should be addressed to Ernest Hirschbach, 129 16th Avenue, Two Mountains, Quebec J7R 3X6.

99

there exist some children—not too many, but some—whom we cannot understand and cannot reach with the tools we have today. Frustration builds up when workers try to treat children whom they cannot treat; that pressure can cause a worker to abuse an untreatable child or other childen. Obviously, violence is not an appropriate reaction. Instead, we need to know who these "unreachable" children are and try to find new strategies for dealing with them.

We have found no literature subscribing to the premise that there are "inaccessible children." Finlay and Randall seem convinced that there are no "untreatable adolescents" (1975). The Laidlaw Workshop on the "Impossible Child" gives definitions and descriptions for management and treatment of severely disturbed children but falls short of designating any of these categories of children as inaccessible (1978). Obviously, this first attempt to examine the question is unlikely to produce any definite answers to acceptable solutions. If this article can become a basis for a full, honest, and compassionate debate on the seriousness of the problem and the validity of our concern, its purpose will be achieved.

Almost 20 years ago, we admitted into one of the group homes of a Montreal children's service agency a 15-year-old girl with a history of Hodgkin's disease that had been in remission for several years. After she had had her physical examination, our pediatrician asked me with some hesitation: "Are you aware that this girl will never see her 21st birthday?"

I was shocked; I had never encountered Hodgkin's before and was unfamiliar with its course. Mary was a pretty, vivacious teenager who had been able to accept her father's desertion and her mother's multiple hospitalizations in a psychiatric hospital reasonably well; she looked forward to group home placement for the next few years until she would finish high school, find a job, and get ready for independent living. Did this girl really have less than 6 years to live?

There is little more to tell about Mary. She blossomed in the group home and was well-liked by her peers and the adults. She graduated from high school with good marks. She obtained interesting employment with good prospects for the future and worked happily for 6 months, buying dishes and material for curtains and saving for the rent payments on that first apartment of her own. Then the disease recurred; all treatment efforts were ineffective, and after 4 months of hospitalization Mary died in the nineteenth year of her life.

The story is tragic, but we can understand and accept it. We know that illness and death are not limited to the old; we also understand that medical science in its present state has no remedies for many diseases.

We can restore, or at least improve, the physical health of some patients suffering from cancer or heart disease; others, as we realize, are incurably ill and will die, even at the age of 19.

However, we extend this awareness and acceptance of the limits of medical knowledge only to the victims of organic disease. In the area of mental and emotional disorders, we do not ever permit ourselves or others to conclude what my pediatrician told me: "There is no known treatment for this illness; we cannot help this child." Why can we accept the limitations of human knowledge in one area but not in another?

Before trying to respond to this question, it seems essential to define the term "treatment." In organic and functional illness, there seem to be basically two reactions to the pathological condition: we can try to cure it, i.e., restore to health, or we can help the patient to adjust to it. Obviously a cure is the preferred treatment, but a diabetic with daily insulin injections and even an amputee with a prosthesis can lead reasonably happy and useful lives and must be considered successfully treated patients.

In child welfare, we are fully aware of the fact that there are many disorders we cannot "cure": the impact of severe childhood deprivation, of multiple placement, of extreme lack of intellectual and emotional stimulation. But frequently we can help a large number of these children to recognize the symptoms and to control the manifestations. Throughout this article we will consider any child "treatable" who can be either restored to health or helped to live reasonably successfully with his or her burden. Untreatable children are only those for whom we can do neither.

Returning to our question, we find at least five substantial reasons for the extreme reluctance of psychiatrists, social workers, and child care workers to accept the premise that, with our present state of understanding of human behavior, we simply do not know how to help some profoundly damaged children.

1. In our knowledge of mental and emotional disorders, we do not possess the same kind of clear, objective body of evidence as is frequently found in our comprehension of organic diseases. In the treatment of functional disorders, we cannot say: this cancer has spread from point A to points B, C, and D and is no longer containable. We cannot say that for a certain condition all applicable medications, surgical interventions, and other therapies have been tried and found ineffective. In our work with children, we always hope that continuation or change of treatment might bring about an improvement; we frequently seem to detect, or perhaps we just imagine, some slight indication of movement. A period of remission implies progress to us and stimulates us to additional efforts.

2. Looking again to medical science as a model, we constantly search for new insights and new therapies that might be the key to the treatment of the apparently untreatable child. Just as the prognosis for Hodgkin's disease was not quite as dismal in 1979 as it was 20 years ago, so do we hope for new treatment modalities for our inaccessible children. But commendable as this search is, does it justify continuing to work with a totally inaccessible child today in the hope that next year, or perhaps in 5 years, new insights and new therapies may be found? One of the complicating factors has been the enormous proliferation of treatment methods (some of them perhaps merely treatment fads) during the past decade. Since the definitions of the types of children who can profit from each program are rather vague at times, the temptation is great to entertain the hope that, even if behavior modification does not benefit Johnny, group psychotherapy or positive peer culture or a therapeutic foster family environment might bring better results.

3. As social workers and child care workers, particularly those in residential settings, get to know a child more intimately, it becomes more and more distressing for them to decide that therapeutic interventions have been attempted long enough and that the time has come to face our inability to help a child. Does one give up after 6 months? After 3 years? At what point? We discover, perhaps to our own surprise, that we are not just detached therapists, but also concerned human beings who have come to be fond of Johnny and are loathe to write him off.

4. We are apprehensive that once we accept the concept of untreatability, it might be used as a justification for not making every possible effort to help the child, so that eventually "untreatability" becomes a self-fulfilling prophecy. This is a valid concern, but it is unreasonable to reject a concept because it is susceptible to abuse. We simply have to be on our guard against this danger.

5. Perhaps the most compelling reason for our reluctance to discontinue treatment is the difficulty of making alternate plans. Unless a reasonably acceptable substitute facility for the care and management of the child can be found, no conscientious child welfare worker will abandon his or her role as the therapist and possibly the guardian of a child.

Which children are inaccessible? They are very difficult to classify because mental, emotional, and social deviations cannot be defined precisely or measured accurately. A pragmatic definition might be simply the classification of a child as "inaccessible" after serious, professional, and diverse treatments in a number of settings over a reasonable period of time have not resulted in any amelioration of the child's problems.

Obviously, this is an imprecise and insufficient definition. We need to make a first, perhaps crude attempt to list some of the categories of children who seem to be least accessible to the efforts of today's child welfare. Before enumerating the three categories of potentially inaccessible children, however, a powerful word of caution: I strongly dislike classifying any group of children. We are too prone to ignore the fact that all children are individuals who react in their own disparate ways to their life experiences. We all know siblings who have been brought up by the same parents in the same environment but who have reacted totally differently to the selfsame happenings. Before listing the categories, it should be emphasized as strongly as possible that they merely provide possible suggestions for the chance that the child, through life experience, may have become inaccessible to treatment.

And even though it seems self-evident, we should perhaps underscore that treatment for today's inaccessible child might become attainable in a few years. This article can only deal with our competence in 1980. In 1985, a cure for Hodgkin's disease might be found, but Mary died because during her illness, no treatment was known.

Within this framework, we want to describe the following three phenomena which seem likely to engender severely disturbed children, inaccessible to the treatment modalities which child welfare can offer today.

1. Children who have been exposed to severe early and prolonged deprivations in their childhood, both physical and emotional deprivations, and show most of the characteristics of this syndrome: severe inability to form lasting and meaningful interpersonal relationships, inability to control a violent temper, destructive tendencies toward self or others, complete withdrawal from social relations.

2. The ill-defined socio-emotional syndrome which is now labeled as "severe character disorder" and in simpler days was called "psychopathic personality." We can describe such children as asocial or without superego, recognizing perfectly well that this categorization indicates little solid understanding of causation and dynamics and practically no concept of treatment. One must caution that, as Wolman points out, severe depression following abandonment or deprivation can also mask itself as an "affectless, psychopathic character" (1972).

3. Children whose capacity and propensity to relate to others have been systematically destroyed by a multitude of placement changes throughout their childhood.

Undoubtedly other categories of severely damaged children, inaccessible to the treatment methods available today, could be added to this list.

Barker describes from the literature other—mostly related—groups: the "unintegrated," the "frozen" child, and the "archipelago" (Laidlaw Workshop, 1978). The applicable common denominator is the inability of therapists to reach them and to help them to effect any change.

One other group of children which probably could be regarded as "untreatable" needs only perfunctory attention because it is very small and of little significance in the established child welfare programs. These are the patients who manage to survive as long as they remain in therapy. Their adjustment is precarious, and they can function only with regular and fairly intensive therapeutic assistance, but as long as this is available, the patient is enabled to hang on. In our presentation, we are ignoring the small number of "lifers."

Anybody who had read this article to this point and agrees with its premise that the inaccessible child exists and presents a major child welfare problem is bound to ask now, "But what do I do about such a child if right now he or she is my responsibility?" The worker might even express it more crudely: "The terminal cancer patient dies eventually and thereby solves the hospital's problem of caring for a person who is beyond therapeutic intervention, but our "terminal patients" go on living, abusing our facilities without benefiting in any way from them. What can be done?"

In trying to answer this crucial question, we must begin by accepting the premise that some children do exist for whom—with our present body of knowledge of human behavior—we can do nothing constructive, nothing helpful; they sabotage treatment plans, disorganize the group home, reject casework and psychiatric intervention. We have not yet found any responses that are fully satisfactory: there are no panaceas, no easy answers.

The most serious problem these children present is their inability to tolerate treatment modalities that in any way attempt to control their impulsive behavior. They are incapable of anticipating the consequences of their actions and of letting themselves be guided by this foreknowledge. It is easy enough to demand the formulation of a plan that takes this inability into consideration, but society is unwilling to tolerate individuals who totally and continuously disregard the rights and feelings of everybody around them. When dealing with such persons, we are forced to weigh the welfare of a group of people—parents and siblings of the client, the other residents and the child care workers in an institution or a group home, teacher and children in a classroom—against the rights and the needs of this one inaccessible child. We will have to accept the fact that at present we do not have any treatment modalities that can be helpful to such children, but that their presence and their actions are harmful to the clients and personnel of any treatment facility. We submit that most children whom we describe as "untreatable" show us quite clearly that their resistance to all of our treatment programs is complete: they run away from residential treatment, escape from "security" institutions, and sabotage an Outward Bound Program.

Furthermore, there is the question of funds. Even though it is to be hoped that we will not always have to work under the prevailing severe budgetary restrictions, it still seems to be extremely questionable whether any society should pay out very large amounts of money for children with very doubtful prognoses while, at the same time, the promising child and the average child are treated pretty niggardly in child welfare budgets. It is almost incomprehensible to reconcile a per diem cost of $250 for a child in a specialized treatment center with board rates for children in foster homes that are a wretchedly small fraction of this amount. Perhaps we need to examine our priorities on this issue.

Our task, therefore, is to design a setting offering only the most basic services under an irreducible minimum of clear, uncomplicated rules, with the supreme commandment clearly stated and uncompromisingly enforced: "If you cannot abide by our few rules, you will be removed immediately. You can return tomorrow, but unless you are then ready to comply, you will not be allowed to remain tomorrow, either."

We propose two measures:

1. The creation of the position of special advocate for each inaccessible child. This advocate is not perceived as occupying a position of authority and is not involved in the process that determines the discontinuation of treatment. He or she is seen as a stable and constant advisor who remains concerned and ready to help wherever the child may reside. The advocate clarifies and interprets but does not make decisions or judgments; he or she is available whenever requested but does not reach out.

2. The establishment of open, loosely structured hostel-type settings that aim only to provide the basic necessities of life, namely, the essential requirements of food, shelter, and clothing, with very clear and strictly enforced limits of tolerance of antisocial behavior: no drugs or alcohol; no verbal or physical violence towards staff or residents' persons, property, or self-respect; no aimless "hanging around" the building. The consequence of violating this code is immediate but temporary expulsion.

Opportunities should be provided to earn goods or money beyond the basic assistance offered by the setting, again under clear and strictly stipulated conditions: for instance, satisfactory performance of a work program, participation in educational or rehabilitative programs, or a specific period without hostile encounters with residents or staff of the facility could all be rewarded.

No discussion and absolutely no argument over the client's behavior should be tolerated by use of the simple and hard-boiled approach: "What we say, goes; accept it or leave! You can discuss anything with your special advocate."

The total strategy should clearly indicate to the clients that society still cares and is still ready to meet their minimal needs, but on a firmly reciprocal basis:

> If you want something from us, this is the price you must pay, and pay immediately upon delivery of the goods. No free lunch, no deferred payments. If you can manage to participate in our program without disrupting it, we are willing to maintain a tenuous, watchful relationship with you from which we will withdraw as soon as you revert to the behavior which previously forced us to consider you untreatable. But you can always come back on the following day and try again on the same basis.

Before I am accused of being cruel and vindictive and expelled from my professional associations, I would like to compare my proposed solution—admittedly a rigid and uncompromising approach—with the way in which many of us now solve the dilemma of inaccessible children and their impact on our settings. At present, we do not label these young people "untreatable," but actually, incapable of managing them in our facilities, we are frustrated into abusing them, we return them to the courts, or we breathe a sigh of relief when they run away; in other words, we wash our hands of them, hoping that they, along with their problems, will disappear forever. What we suggest here is a first attempt—undoubtedly crude, perhaps oversimplified—to try dealing with a situation that we have dodged and ignored too often. We are fully aware of the limitations of our approach: a good number of the angry and alienated young people will resent the "take-it-or-leave-it" attitude of the proposed hostel; they will reject it and submerge themselves in the subculture of the alienated: drugs, hand-to-mouth living, constant change of domicile. Yet they are doing that now, too; the difference will be that whereas now we simply abandon the unreachable teenager and close our doors quite firmly, the hostel, with all its rigid structures, will always hold out a hand of welcome. "If you are ready to comply with our few basic standards, we are ready to meet your basic needs today or tomorrow or in 6 months."

The vehement advocates of children's rights undoubtedly will not care for this concept, but we would like to advance two points for their consideration. One is that no bill of rights can enjoin physicians to heal their patients or social workers to cure their clients. We all work within the boundaries of our knowledge and our competence. Secondly, children's rights, as the rights of any conceivable segment of society, are not absolute; they are circumscribed and must be so limited by the needs, the rights, and the limitations of the total community. On a lifeboat one might say, "I am thirsty, therefore I will drink until my thirst is quenched, even though there is an allotment of two ounces of water per day for every one of us." Yet even the law recognizes self-preservation as an overriding necessity and permits the passengers in the lifeboat to remove the threat of their existence by throwing the transgressor overboard.

It is obvious that our design is an inadequate, at best partial, solution, but in our opinion it is an improvement over the present situation that denies and conceals the problem. There are many other quandaries in human relations which, at present, we are solving rather inadequately. Locking up criminals has proven to be not only inhumane but also ineffective; nevertheless, we continue this futile performance because we lack preferable alternatives. "Awarding'" children from a broken marriage to one or the other of the two partners creates as many problems as it solves. The sad fact is that so far we simply have not found any satisfactory answers to these problems. We have to accept the proposition—and social workers find this very difficult—that in many areas of human relationships there exist situations which we cannot solve adequately; all we can do is to find the least detrimental response.

In summary, there are some groups of children whose life experiences have damaged them so severely that they can no longer be reached by the therapeutic interventions we know today but respond negatively and with hostility to all of our efforts. Since their attitude endangers the accessible child in our child welfare settings, new ways to coping with the "child beyond reach" must be found.

REFERENCES

Finley, D., & Randall, D. Treating the untreatable adolescent. *Canada's Mental Health*, September 1975, *23*,3.

Laidlaw Workshop on The Impossible Child. *Supplement to Canadian Psychiatric Association Journal*, December 1978, *23*, SS.

Wolman, B. B. (Ed.). *Manual of child psychopathology*. McGraw-Hill, 1972.

RESPONSES TO THE PROBLEM

NO ONE WILL THANK YOU:
FIRST THOUGHTS ON REPORTING
INSTITUTIONAL ABUSE

Roderick Durkin

ABSTRACT. The author gives advice to those who could bring charges of abuse against an institution and speaks of the standards that cannot be compromised by not bringing charges. He points out that the institution will defend itself and that the accuser should be sure of the facts and have a plan of action with alternative strategies. Reports that he points out can be made internally or externally but must in all cases consider the need of the child for protection.

Since a specific incident of abuse by an individual worker in an institutional setting (or by a parent in a family) is often the result of many circumstances within the institution, accusations of child abuse against an individual are commonly viewed as attacks on the entire institution. The resistance to such reports, therefore, tends to be strong, and the institutions which would welcome them tend to be those that are not likely to have high rates of abuse. Institutions' responses to such external attack may include reactions similar to those manifested in families identified or accused of abuse: denial, cover-up action, or defensive behavior. The motivations for "avoiding" the problems are also similar. The accused will fear punishment or reprisal, want to protect reputations and careers,

Roderick Durkin is Director of Research, Seattle Day Nursery Association, 302 Broadway, Seattle, WA 98122. Requests for reprints should be addressed to the author, P.O. Box 57, Jamaica, VT 04343.

try to cover the deed to serve the long-term needs of the social unit (family or institution), and be unwilling to acknowledge the presence of internal factors that lead to child abuse. Whatever the powerful forces that evoke abusive behavior, professional training and understanding do not assure the taking of prompt, positive, and appropriate action.

Invdividuals who suspect (or know) that institutional child abuse is occurring may have valid concerns about reporting incidents, which explains their frequent reticence. Such concerns may be personal in nature, such as the fear of losing their jobs or the desire to avoid becoming involved in what is usually a messy business at best, or may reflect attitudes regarding the system, be it the county Children's Protective Service agency or the institution, which may be ineffective or bureaucratic. Regardless of these factors, this article emphasizes each individual's ethical and professional responsibility—and legal obligation—to report incidents of possible abuse.

Most state laws mandate reporting by medical, education, social service, and law enforcement professionals and grant legal immunity from prosecution for libel and slander when acting in good faith in reporting incidents. Failure to report child abuse can result in misdemeanor charges in many states, and professionals must recognize this as a possibility when deciding how to report a suspected child abuse case. Beyond the legal considerations, the ethical and professional standards which cannot be compromised when considering how to proceed include:

1. Institutions that claim to be experts in caring for children, guiding them, and promoting appropriate behavior should never resort to physical or psychological abuse, and no set of circumstances within the institution should be so severe as to provoke such behavior on the part of the staff. The old medical dictum, "First, do no harm!" applies here as well. Furthermore, sexual abuse of children in institutions is particularly inadmissible because institutional life may preclude any meaningful ability to withhold consent to sexual activity on the child's part.

2. People working with children have a professional responsibility to protect children in their care, and the rights of those children should not be compromised in any way. Professionals must report child abuse despite the possibility that it may endanger their jobs or the institution, and institutions must accept this position no matter what the consequences are. This mandate does not, of course, license an individual to destroy individuals or institutions for personal reasons.

3. If abuse does occur, children must be given a candid explanation of the events, including their own involvement, and they must be debriefed. Too many children who have had bad experiences in institutions are fearful and distrust those who could provide the help that constitutes the only justification for their being there in the first place. In short, institutions and the professionals who work in them need to admit candidly where they erred and to help minimize the long term consequences of the abuse for the child.

How to Report Abuse

A first step in preparing to report an incident of abuse is to ascertain the facts. Who, how, when, where, and why did the abuse occur? It is essential to be reasonably sure that the incident did, in fact, occur, lest individuals be blamed unfairly. However, one should always err on the side of caution and take action which will protect the child. If the incident is doubtful, one should perhaps proceed less aggressively, particularly if there are no witnesses or corroborative material.

Internal Vs. External Reporting

Once one is convinced that abuse has occurred, the next step is to assess the situation and anticipate which method of reporting will be most effective in remedying similar and future situations. Determining which channel to utilize is a complex and imprecise process. The legal mandate to report can be considered an external mechanism. Under this system, a report is filed with Child Protective Services, which is normally empowered to record the incident and to investigate and take action to protect the child. It appears that this is the most logical place to report an incident if the institution is unresponsive to the needs of children, prone to protect itself, and seems to value institutional survival and the careers of its staff ahead of the rights of children. CPS may also prove useful if the problems of abuse are recurring or widespread, if the reporter has no support system within the institution, or if he or she has little or no power or status within the institution.

Depending partly on local legal requirements, of course, an individual may choose to handle the matter internally, at least at first, by going directly to the supervisor or the agency director. This is most frequently an effective action if the institution has a history of being open to criticism or change, if the incident appears to be an isolated one, if the professional reporting the incident is well-respected or has status or credibility in the institution and with the administration, or if it is determined that CPS will be unable to take effective action. The latter may reflect some bureaucratic "favoritism" for or allegiance to the institution, administration, or larger system (e.g., public welfare or state hospital system).

There are both risks and benefits to consider when determining which approach (or which combination) seems likely to be most effective, and these factors often determine what course of action, if any, a professional should take in reporting an incidence of abuse. While reporters are granted legal immunity if they report, there are no guarantees of immunity from harassment from colleagues and administration. Choosing to handle the matter through internal channels may earn the appreciation of the institution if it is sincere in its concern for young people in its care or trying to protect its public image, but there is always the possibility that the reporter will lose his or her job—or be made to feel so uncomfortable as to be forced to leave. This can occur as a result of either internal or external reporting and is almost assured if the reporter chooses to call in the media—an option that should be viewed as only a last resort.

There is no one solution or one "right" way of reporting incidents of abuse, and thus reporters are encouraged to consider all possible options. Depending on the circumstances, it may be wise for the reporters to make clear to the institution how they will proceed if the matter is not or cannot be handled internally. If one method is not effective, it may be necessary to use an alternative one.

Regardless of the direction an individual decides to take, the possibility remains that no internal action will be taken. This is particularly likely in an institution which is hoping to ignore or cover up the incident. While there is no assurance that external reporting will be any more effective, at a minimum Child Protective Services is mandated to make a written record of reported incidents.

Responding to Allegations of Abuse

In all instances the overriding concern must be for the protection of the abused child, and action must be designated not only to protect the child from possible attempts by staff or peers to exact retribution, but also to safeguard the rights and dignity of the alleged abuser. To balance the rights of the child and those of the alleged abuser, everyone should be heard and their stories given due consideration. The incident should be explored openly, candidly, and in as nonthreatening a manner as possible. Depending on the amount of evidence available, the alleged abuser may be suspended pending a hearing. An example of this process is provided in the following excerpt from an actual case:

> In a rural work farm resident treatment program for delinquent boys, two boys alleged that a popular staff member, who had been at the institution for many years, had used them homosexually. The boys were interrogated independently by the director who determined that the incident probably had occurred since the circumstances were similar and there was corroborating evidence. When the staff member was confronted, he denied the accusation, alleging that the boys were getting even for another grievance. The director suspended the man immediately pending a more thorough investigation. At the suggestion of a consultant, the director set up a committee that included friends of the accused to review the case.

If it is determined that the alleged abuse actually occurred, of course, there may be justification for discharge and, depending on the circumstance, legal action.

Some Final Thoughts on Reporting

Professionals who report incidents of child abuse must be prepared to expect defensive reactions or counterattacks from the institution and administration; as in the old Russian proverb, "Sometimes you will eat the bear and sometimes the bear will eat you." The professional and ethical standards provide a guideline for action; to follow them, one must develop an effective strategy for reporting each case, pressing for an investigation and persevering until the situation is corrected. Reporters must be aware of their options, their support, and the strength of their contentions.

Those who report will find the first experience of bringing charges of child abuse to be the hardest. They need active supporters or, at least, confidants. The experience is difficult and lonely, particularly when it threatens job security and future employment. However, if children's services are to continue, we must provide quality child care free from abuse and neglect. It is the further responsibility of professionals to improve the overall quality of services and to change the conditions that lead to institutional child abuse.

DIRECT CARE WORKERS' ATTITUDES TOWARD USE OF PHYSICAL FORCE WITH CHILDREN

Nolan Rindfleisch
Joan Baros-Van Hull

ABSTRACT. Nolan Rindfleisch used role-playing techniques in a survey to examine factors influencing the use of force with children in institutions. The study describes several factors associated with the willingness to use force, among them the amount of resentment toward children, the management of routines in the organization, the amount of staff participation in decison making in the facility, the size of the community in which the direct care giver was reared, and the age of the care giver. The writers suggest some methods for preventing and managing use of force and some implications for future research.

Introduction

Injury to children resulting from physical force is a social phenomenon that has attracted intense public and scientific interest in the last 10-15 years. While use of physical force in child care has been seen primarily as occurring within the home, Gil (1975) argued that physical force is also to be found at the institutional and societal levels. The institutional level includes settings such as day care centers, schools, courts, child welfare agencies, welfare departments, and correctional and other residential child settings.

Current national awareness and concern about the problem of child abuse and neglect in residential facilities has been generated through advocacy activities, litigation, and legislation. As a result, attention has

Nolan Rindfleisch is Associate Professor, College of Social Work, The Ohio State University, Columbus, OH 43210. Joan Baros-Van Hull is also affiliated with the College of Social Work, The Ohio State University. This article is a summary of the findings of Nolan Rindfleisch's (1976, 1978) dissertation. Requests for reprints should be addressed to Nolan Rindfleisch at the above address.

often focused on deficiencies in particular facilities, rather than on understanding the causes of child abuse and neglect in the institution.

Conceptions of the problem vary widely, and much available knowledge about determinants of quality group care is not being used systematically in everyday practice. Because of a widespread tendency to avoid dealing with it, limited information has been developed to guide practitioners at all levels in the residential care field in managing this problem.

Recent research studies do not assist in understanding the nature of abuse and neglect in institutional settings, since writers view the problem almost exclusively in terms of parental inadequacy and personality deviance. Some assert that persons who abuse children were themselves abused (e.g., Jayaratne, 1977). Other writers (e.g., Zigler, 1976) assert that the single most important determinant of child abuse is the willingness of adults to inflict corporal punishment on children in the name of discipline. In addition, studies which examine incidence of child abuse generally omit child caretakers outside the family, e.g., caretakers of children in public and private institutions.

State child abuse reporting laws have also tended to adopt a narrow definition of which caretakers can be considered abusers. These laws have, as a result, focused attention on force used within the home.

In attempting to understand child abuse and neglect at the institutional level, factors such as age, education, and personality of care givers along with the use of force in institutions are seen as important contributors to the mistreatment of children. Participants at the National Conference on Institutional Abuse in June of 1977 found that the following factors may contribute to abuse and neglect in institutions: large size of the institution, inadequate staffing, isolation from community and family, limited public awareness, inadequate regulations, and the limited availability of appropriate alternatives to residential care.

Purpose of the Study

The present study was undertaken to examine attitudes of direct caregivers in children's homes toward the use of physical force with children and to determine factors associated with variations in levels of force found justifiable by direct care givers. This study utilized a view of institutional abuse that was multicausal, since it was felt that several factors influence the occurrence of abuse in such settings. It was designed to shed light on the source and dynamics of child abuse in the institutions and hopefully provide a foundation for developing approaches to the prevention and control of physical abuse at the institutional level.

Theoretical Background

In exploring social factors which shape and generate violence against children, a theoretical analysis of violence between intimates (Goode, 1973) was used as a framework for this study. This model underlines the powerful roles of (1) *norms*, in creating differential chances of violence; (2) *social pressures and structural position*, in creating differential chances of violence among people with different predispositions; and (3) *a sense of injustice*, as a dynamic through which violence is generated.

Underlying the relationships predicted between variables derived from this model were several assumptions:

1. All social systems require a minimum degree of control and order if they are to survive, and physical force is one of several means that can be used to achieve them.

2. Those who control service organizations make a distinction between the wishes and interests of their beneficiaries. A divisiveness exists between beneficiaries and organizations which sometimes results in hostility and conflict.

3. Service organizations must develop mechanisms to cope with self-activating properties of clients in order to insure that change activities are not rendered ineffective.

4. Children's homes are, in part, force-based structures, and use of physical force is a resource available to them as they seek to achieve their objectives.

The factors in this study were those which accounted for varying predispositions to use of force in care giving. They are the status variables which available demographic analysis suggest to be characteristic of certain violence-prone collectivities. They constitute the sociocultural context within which force use occurs.

Social pressures and structural position were defined as the extent to which management practices are institution- or resident-oriented, the degree of staff participation in organization decision making, and the degree of control over the immediate work environment (Holland, 1973; Thomas, 1975).

Care giver-child relationships were viewed in this study as a form of social exchange. When what care givers receive from children over a period of time is seen by them as not roughly proportional to what they have given, feelings of distress gradually build up. We call this distress "injustice distress." Sense of injustice is a dynamic through which use of force is generated. This factor was seen as exerting a direct influence on the level of force espoused by care givers (Singleman, 1972).

Method and Sample

The study utilized a survey design to examine the relationship between a number of social factors and attitudes of direct care givers toward use of physical force on children.

One hundred direct care givers in 42 living units in 15 central and southwestern Ohio children's homes for dependent, neglected, and disturbed children were included. Twenty-five direct care givers were selected from each of the following categories: small public (under 50 children), small private, large public (over 50), and large private institutions.

The instrument was a self-administered questionnaire consisting of five parts: Part I contained questions about the institution; Part II included questions about the care giver's job and background; Part III contained questions about how to deal with several hypothetical child care situations presented through verbal descriptions and graphic depictions; Part IV was composed of questions about participation in decision making. Centralization in decision making was measured by use of a scale developed by Aiken and Hage (1968). It consisted of two subscales: staff participation in organization decision making and staff control over their immediate work environment. Part V contained questions about how children are actually managed in the living unit. The extent to which resident management practices are institution- or resident-oriented was measured by a scale developed by King and Raynes (1968).

The hypothetical child care situations presented in the questionnaire were varied in terms of the amounts of challenge presented by the child's behavior in each. Direct care givers were asked to indicate how often they would take each of six possible actions. One of these possible actions was, "Take no physical action at all." They were also asked to state how much resentment they would be likely to feel if they were the care givers in the hypothetical situations. Responses were made on a 5-point scale from "none" to a "great deal" (Blumenthal, 1972).

The effects of age and sex of the children were controlled by including only boys under 14 in the situations and care givers of boys under 14 in the sample.

The Findings

Characteristics of Direct Care Givers

The group of direct care givers surveyed was composed of 37 men and 63 women. This ratio is not atypical of the human service field generally. However, the distribution of ages of direct care givers was probably unique to the residential group care field, since 35% of the direct care givers were under 25, while another 38% were over 45 years of age. What is largely absent from this profile of staff is the 30-45 age range, the one into which most of the parents of residents probably fall.

There is evidence that many direct care givers are new to this field and occupation. Forty-one had been in their present job 1 year or less, and 59 indicated that the present job was their first in the field. Thirty direct care givers had been in their present position for 4 years or more.

Forty-four direct care givers had never been married, while 56 were married or had been married. One implication of this is that a substantial portion of direct care givers had no experience in being a parent.

While 42% of the direct care givers had attended school for 12 years or less, most had had some college or graduate work. In a state where there are no standards regarding minimum education qualifications for the direct care job, it is interesting to note that one in three direct care givers had at least a college degree.

Factors Associated with Willingness to Use Force

Factors associated with the willingess of direct care givers to consider using force to deal with challenges presented by residents were examined in this study. There were 19 items in all which seemed to influence, in varying degrees, the likelihood that more rather than less force would be used to deal with these situations.

It was thought that factors such as the amount of resentment toward a child that the direct care giver feels, the extent to which the direct care giver is acted upon by a centralized, organization-centered administration, along with the region and place (urban/rural) in which direct care givers were reared, would influence the likelihood that more or less force would be espoused in dealing with situations presented in the institution. Several of these factors were found to be strongly or moderately associated with the direct care giver's willingness to use force to deal with the challenges of children in care.

It was found that the amount of force selected by direct care givers to manage the challenging child care situations could be expected to increase if they were older, had a lower amount of educational training, were or had been married, were reared in a smaller community, participated seldom or never in decision making in the facility, "lived in" on a 24-hour basis, worked in a living unit where the activities of everyday life were not managed in resident-oriented ways (more attention given to resident needs than to meeting the needs of the organization), and experienced a higher degree of resentment toward the children.

Since each factor was associated to some extent with every other factor, the data were examined to determine which would independently be most strongly associated with willingness to use force with children. Five factors were found to be uniquely associated with willingness to use force:

1. Amount of resentment toward the children;
2. Management of routines of everyday life in an organization-centered way;
3. Seldom or never participating in decision making in the facility;
4. Size of the community in which the direct care giver was reared; and
5. Age of the care giver.

The association of all factors taken together for the entire group with the willingness to use force on children was $R = .63$.

When these five factors were related to the willingness of direct care givers to use force on children separately for women and men in the sample, some interesting results were suggested. While the level of significance obtained for each subgroup was greater than .05, the multiple correlation obtained for women was $R = .63$ and that for men was $R = .79$. These results suggest that the factors included in this study reflect better the influences affecting men's willingness to use force on children than they do women's. This difference between men and women in the sample may be due to differential socialization of men and women. It may be due, in part, to the reluctance of women respondents to select moderate to high force levels because of their concern that making such choices would reflect negatively on them as women.

Data indicated that those who were reared in smaller towns and those who were older were more predisposed to use force on children. Other studies (Krause, 1974; Raynes, 1975) have concluded that background variables were not significantly related to the care giver behavior measured. In view of these findings, the fact that older respondents tended to justify higher levels of force stands out as exceptional.

Younger direct care givers were not as willing to use force on children. This could be interpreted as an effect of uncertainty in their roles, of having come to maturity in a period of "permissiveness," and of having higher levels of education. The higher levels of willingness to use force by older care givers can be interpreted as an effect of their having come to maturity at an earlier period, when use of force was widely supported in the society as a normal means in care giving. The sample was characterized by a substantial presence of care givers under 25 and over 45 years of age. Differences between these two groups in educational level, reasons for being in the field, previous work experience, and attitudes toward the care-giver job suggest that the field is attracting two quite distinct types of staff. The younger group may be more numerous in the private field, while the older group may be more numerous in the public field. However, the younger care givers seem to remain for shorter periods in the job: given this circumstance, the question should be posed as to whether the younger care givers would express the same willingness to use force if they were to continue in their jobs beyond 4 years.

Implications for Practice

Management Issues

Decentralization of decision making and more resident-centered management practices were found to contribute to lower levels of consideration of the use of physical force. An implication of this finding is that program changes that lead to increasing care givers' participation in decision making and to individualizing children's care will lower the amount of force likely to be used.

Based on our findings about the influence of resentment on level of force, we suggest that care giving may flow less from generosity and concern with the needs of children, but more on the basis of the care giver's feelings of equity and inequity resulting from the exchange between him/herself and the children. It should be recalled that respondents were to deal with given child care situations. One alternative was to take no physical action at all. Respondents could have chosen to do nothing or break off with the child. That respondents chose physical actions suggests that they felt such strong resentment that they did not perceive other alternatives as viable, given the situation as they experienced it.

These results reflect what is classically defined as "burnout." Burnout is characterized by such symptoms as hostility toward clients and agency, apathy, detachment of oneself from client problems and duties on the job, negativism, lack of attentiveness, increased absenteeism, cynicism, and little motivation to perform well on the job. Burnout is typically associated in the human services field with work in high-stress situations.

Our data suggest that care givers also deal with their inequity distress by leaving their jobs. The likelihood that direct care givers under the age of 34 would be in their jobs for less than 4 years was very high. Our presumption in the case of younger care givers is that this is a factor in their shorter periods of tenure. The influence of this distress on younger care givers was illustrated by one direct care giver who reported that she was completely drained and would be leaving the home in 3 months. The expectation that she soon would be leaving her position, after just 1 year on the job, seemed to enable her to make it through her shifts (Berry, 1975).

These findings are consistent with the findings of Erlanger (1974) and Kohn (1969), who analyzed the influence of stress on the levels of physical force used by care givers from lower social segments. They agree that the conformity orientation of lower status care givers can be viewed as a consequence of limited education and constricting job conditions.

The interrelation of these factors in the case of older workers is exemplified in an anecdote reported by another direct care giver:

> An older care giver with over 4 years tenure, contrary to a home rule, used considerable force to control a boy in his living unit. He took the boy to the superintendent and said, "Support me in what I did; if you do not, the boy is yours, I'm leaving."

Consistent with the results of our study, but not dependent on them, are some suggestions which administrators might consider to reduce the likelihood of physical force being used:

1. There is some indication that the relative isolation of a 24-hour live-in schedule may be related to willingness to use force. Steps should be taken both to enhance the autonomy of staff working in this pattern and

to balance this with assurance of support as the direct care giver organizes the activities of everyday life in the living unit.

2. Deployment of care givers should be planned so that more staff are in the living unit during peak hours. Care-giver "backup" should be provided at all times.

3. To counter feelings of being drained, or "burned out," an equivalent of the military "rest and rehabilitation" procedures should be considered.

Personnel Issues

Our findings revealed that the older direct care giver (age 45 and above) was more willing to consider the use of force on children in the institution. Thus, in agency hiring procedures, it would be desirable for an agency to establish minimum educational qualifications. High school completion would change the age distribution of care givers in the field in the direction of the younger categories. Younger direct care givers did not expresss a willingness to use force as readily as the older direct care giver.

Another alternative administrators should consider is to offer more in-service training that addresses such issues as child development, dynamics of abuse and neglect, working with children, and methods of controlling children.

Implications for Research

Further light could be shed on the dynamics of institutional abuse through replication of this study. Researchers who might choose to replicate this work should plan their work with awareness of the limitations of this research.

First, we note the inherent difficulty in studying what has been called "voluntary harm-doing." Laboratory researchers have found it almost impossible to induce respondents to harm others voluntarily. We utilized a role-playing technique because it was shown to produce results very similar to those derived from use of deception. Employment of a surrogate measure for physical force application was also necessary. While the "attitude" we measured was defined as a predisposition to action, we did not conclude that a respondent who chose a high force level would necessarily use high force under all circumstances.

The design of the study was characterized as *ex post facto*. Multiple measures were obtained at one time from a single group of respondents.

While multivariate analysis techniques permitted us to control for known alternatives, we had no control over unknown alternative explanations.

Our sample was purposively drawn, not randomly drawn. Therefore, our findings lack generalizability to any population other than to the 42 living units actually measured in the study. We do not purport to generalize to the 15 homes sampled, since we sought participation of care givers only of those living units which had boys in residence whose average age was 14 years and under. We were constrained in sample selection by the inability of some small public homes to participate due to their low census or to staff absence at the time of data collection.

Since this study used hypothetical situations as a basis for measuring abuse potential, further effort needs to be made to ground future research in validated cases of abuse in institutions. Finally, studies which assess what staff actions or institutional conditions are perceived as more or less severe forms of abuse and neglect are also needed.

Summary

In summary, use of a research approach that analyzes the relationship between a number of factors taken together and level of force used should be of considerable assistance in extending our understanding of the sources and dynamics of violence against children. This research approach should also help in the development of effective approaches to preventing and managing this phenomenon, especially as it is manifested at the institutional level.

REFERENCES

Berry, J. *Daily experience in residential life*. Boston: Routledge and Kegan Paul, Ltd., 1975.

Blumenthal, M., et al. *Justifying violence: Attitudes of American men*. Ann Arbor: Institute of Social Research, The University of Michigan, 1972.

Erlanger, H. Social class and corporal punishment in child rearing: A reassessment. *American Sociological Review*, 1974, *39*, 68-85.

Gil, D. A holistic perspective on child abuse and its prevention. Paper presented at a Conference on Child Abuse and Neglect at National Institute of Child Health and Human Development, 1974.

Goode, W. J. Force and violence in the family. *Journal of Marriage and the Family*, 1971, *33*, 624-636.

Goode, W. *Explorations in social theory*. New York: Oxford University Press, 1973.

Holland, T. Organizational structure and institutional care. *Journal of Health and Social Behavior*, 1973, *14*, 241-251.

Krause, K. Authoritarianism, dogmatism, and coercion in child caring institutions: A study of staff attitudes. *Child Welfare*, 1974, *53*, 23-30.

Raynes, N., Pratt, M. & Roses, S. *Aides involvement in decision making and the quality of care in institutional settings.* Unpublished Report, 1975.

Rindfleisch, N. J. *A study of the influence of background and organizational factors on direct care workers' attitudes toward use of physical force on children.* Unpublished doctoral dissertation, Ohio State University, 1976.

Rindfleisch, N J. A study of the influence of background and organizational factors on direct care workers' attitudes toward use of physical force on children. *Dissertation Abstracts,* 1978, *38* (8).

Singleman, P. Exhange as symbolic interaction: Convergences between two sociological perspectives. *American Sociological Review,* 1972, *37,* 414-472.

Thomas, G. *The effectiveness of child caring institutions.* Regional Institute of Social Welfare Research. Athens: University of Georgia, 1975.

CLOSING THE BARN DOOR: THE PREVENTION OF INSTITUTIONAL ABUSE THROUGH STANDARDS

Marc Mercer

ABSTRACT. The author says that institutional abuse is best prevented by designing programs according to acceptable standards instead of by investigating on a case-by-case basis. He uses a new set of guidelines to illustrate prevention theory, good staffing and supervision, careful programming, involvement of outside community members, and regulated discipline methods.

The present focus on institutional abuse, as reflected in the recent proliferation of conferences and articles on the subject, is welcomed by all those who are concerned about the quality of the lives of children placed in residential facilities. There is, however, the concern that this focus will not promote a comprehensive understanding of the complex problems of residential care.

Institutional abuse is, according to this view, a symptom of much else that is wrong in facilities with serious patterns of abuse. Solutions addressing this symptom, while they may have great value, are unlikely to have a significant impact on those conditions within the facility which encourage abuse of children. Current approaches generally stress reporting, investigation, and correction of incidents. Such approaches, however necessary, are only means of closing the barn door after the horse is gone, in the words of the old saying.

Programs designed to educate people in the field about the problem are subject to similar objections. Though it is very positive to have an open dialogue on a subject long suppressed in professional circles, such a dia-

Marc Mercer is Staff Writer for the Interstate Consortium on Residential Child Care, Capital Place One, 222 South Warren Street, CN 700, Trenton, NJ 08625. The views expressed are based on the author's interpretation of the new set of residential care standards developed by this group and do not constitute official positions of this organization. Requests for reprints should be addressed to Marc Mercer at the above address.

logue is largely useful only in defining the areas where we need to take action.

These important first steps must be followed up by more comprehensive thinking about the problems of residential facilities, about measures to prevent abuse, and finally about positive, rather than negative, constructs for improving the quality of care in residential facilities. A policy toward residential care developed on the basis of what we do not want done to children is, in the absence of all else, a tragic admission of defeat.

We have noted that institutional child abuse is a symptom of serious disorders in a facility that has a serious pattern of abuse. We shall now consider what these disorders might be.

Chief among the causes of abuse is a lack of adequate training and supervision of direct care workers. We might add that a lack of proper screening procedures for staff and economic conditions within the field make it difficult for a facility to attract and retain skilled people. An experienced, well-trained direct care worker always has more options in dealing with a child's behavior than the inexperienced, untrained worker. The experienced worker is much less likely to be in a physical confrontation with a child and, if a confrontation occurs, may be able to handle it without using force. The inexperienced worker is likely to feel frustrated and unsure of control and may try to establish authority in inappropriate ways.

Good supervision prevents abuse in at least two ways. In the first place, supervision involves monitoring employees' actions and state of mind. In the second place, having someone experienced with whom to discuss the problems and pressures of the job makes the workers better able to handle their feelings about the job and the children. We might make the following generalization about the effect of poor personnel practices on the incidence of abuse: facility staff will generally tend to treat children in care as they feel they are treated by the facility administration. An exploitative, unresponsive administration creates an exploitative, unresponsive staff.

As a profession, residential child care is usually grim. Child care jobs are generally dead-end and offer financial rewards at the low end of the scale. Pension plans, health care plans, and similar fringe benefits are available only in some facilities. In general, the message to direct care workers is that they are not particularly valued. All of the rhetoric about the importance of child care cannot obscure this message.

Long hours on the job are one of the major contributing factors. Anyone who has never worked an 80-hour week in a residential program for troubled children would find it hard to understand the emotional state of the worker at the end of one week, looking forward to the next. For one thing, such hours make regular patterns of eating and sleeping impossible. There is no room at all for recreation or a normal social life. Add to this frequent last-minute changes in the schedule and a continuing round of crises and emergencies. After long periods of exposure to these conditions, the normal restraints of the worker's personality may begin to fray.

The facility may contribute to the likelihood of abuse in a variety of other ways. Lack of overall planning and a failure to make behavioral expectations clear to staff and children may be contributing factors. Some facilities lack adequate programmed time and appropriate recreational alternatives. The facility may, in some cases, actually condone certain forms of abuse as a matter of agency policy. Agency policies on use of restraint and of psychotropic medications may, either by omission or commission, encourage abusive acts. In fact, in the sense that every aspect of a facility's program contributes or fails to contribute to a prosocial atmosphere, virtually every aspect of the facility and its program influences the probability of abusive acts.

Throughout this discussion of the causes of abuse, the possibility of a simple solution has become more and more distant. It is as though one of the blind men of the old fable has traced the trunk backward and discovered it to be attached to an elephant. A discussion of the prevention of institutional abuse has led us and will always lead us to a whole complex of issues touching on virtually every aspect of residential programming. This complex of issues might be boiled down to a basic question—what constitutes good, or at least acceptable, residential child care? Comprehensive standards for residential child care would provide, in our opinion, the only complete answer to this question.

The Interstate Consortium on Residential Child Care has been working to develop such standards for the last 2 years. The Consortium is composed of representatives of the purchasers, providers, and regulators of residential care in 14 states, which include Connecticut, Delaware, Maine, Maryland, Massachusetts, New Hampshire, New Jersey, New York, Pennsylvania, Rhode Island, Vermont, Virginia, Washington, D.C., and West Virginia.

The Consortium recently published the *Guidebook on Residential Child Care*. The *Guidebook* includes materials on the responsibilities of government, a proposed set of licensing requirements for residential facilities, guidelines, preferred practices, and extensive commentary on every aspect of the field. At present, Consortium members are seeking implementation of the *Guidebook* in their home states.

One relatively brief section of the *Guidebook* focuses specifically on the question of institutional abuse. This section mandates an internal investigation of abuse, specifies the facility's responsibility to report incidents according to state law, and requires the facility to inform all staff of their responsibility to report abuse. In addition, the facility is required to have procedures to ensure that the staff member involved does not work directly with the child involved during the investigation. This, of course, is not a significant contribution to methods of handling alleged incidents already having occurred.

The Consortium's contribution focuses on the prevention of child abuse through the development and implementation of comprehensive standards for residential care. At this point, we shall attempt to isolate some of the features of this proposed set of standards which would tend not only to protect children from abuse, but also to provide positive constructs for the care and treatment of children.

At the highest level of abstraction, the very notion of a comprehensive set of standards mandating basic levels of performance for *all* residential facilities, regardless of funding source or service provided, increases protection to children experiencing forms of residential care currently subject to lower standards or, for that matter, not currently subject to regulation. At present, the quality of care in a residential facility may be dependent on the funding source, the category of the facility, or a number of other factors basically not relevant to the human needs of the child.

Children in correctional facilities do not, for example, receive the same basic care as childen in mental health facilities. If the Consortium is successful, both types of facilities will be subject to the same standards for basic care, along with additional standards addressing the specific type of care provided. The *Guidebook* provides "core requirements" expressing the standards that would have to be met by all facilities. A series of "modules" provides additional requirements for specialized facilities.

The Consortium believes that one of the major ways of protecting children is by ensuring the continuing involvement of parents, significant others, representatives of involved agencies, and members of the community at large in the residential program. To see the truth of this, we need only consider the major sources of community complaints about abuse. Complaints come from teachers, neighbors, family members, and other persons with whom a child living in the community may come into contact. Children living in institutions, particularly secure institutions, are sometimes isolated from these sorts of contacts. The proposed requirements in the *Guidebook* go to great lengths to combat this kind of isolation. Secure facilities would, for example, be required to have advisory boards of community members. All facilities would be required to have positive strategies for parental and community involvement.

One of the situations with the greatest potential for abuse comes about when staff members who are unclear about their specific responsibilities interact with children who are unclear about the facility's expectations. This situation is frustrating and tension provoking for both parties. The *Guidebook* would require facilities to be very clear about the roles and responsibilities of everyone involved. The facility would have to communicate with both children and staff, clarifying not only rules and routines, but also the rewards for positive behavior and the consequences for negative behavior. The Consortium thinks in terms of a total message to the child, including what the facility wants, as well as what it does not want. We believe this to be an essential precondition for a reasonably safe environment.

The *Guidebook* recognized the direct correlation between the manner in which a facility treats staff and the manner in which these staff will treat the children. For this reason, the proposed standards pay a great deal of attention to personnel practices, orientation, training, and supervision.

The requirements in the *Guidebook* are designed to make residential facilities better workplaces, to ensure proper orientation of new staff members, to ensure continuous training program for staff, and to ensure that staff are properly supervised. The *Guidebook* identifies several critical areas in which all staff must be trained. Chief among these are safety practices and crisis management. Training in crisis management would include instruction in passive physical restraint and nonhurtful methods of stopping children from injuring themselves or others. The *Guidebook* places intelligent control over the methods to be used to treat and manage children. All forms of painful or humiliating punishment are disallowed. More importantly, the facility would be required to have a positive strategy for dealing with children. The facility would establish goals for the program as a whole, for program components, and for individual children, detailing the methods to be used. Periodically, the continued relevance of established goals and the effectiveness of methods would be evaluated.

A lack of programmed recreational and other leisure activities may contibute to a pattern of abuse. Boredom and frustration create friction. The *Guidebook* requires facilities to have both recreational resources and a recreational plan.

The Consortium considers the use of psychotropic medications a major source of potential abuse. There is growing concern in professional circles about the serious side effects sometimes caused by use of these drugs. The *Guidebook* expressly forbids the use of psychotropic drugs as agents for punishment or control. Except in the clearly defined emergency in a secure facility, psychotropic medications would be used only as part of a carefully controlled and carefully monitored therapeutic program. Facilities which use psychotropic medications would be required to maintain a medication counseling program designed to keep children and families informed of the benefits and side effects of particular drugs. The proposed requirements fully recognize the basic rights of children and their parents to be full participants in decisions involving medication.

The use of chemical or mechanical restraint and locked isolation by residential facilities is another matter for concern. The *Guidebook* would restrict the use of such radical procedures to those facilities specifically approved by the regulatory body as "secure care facilities." Use of restraint would only be allowed under specific circumstances. All uses of restraint would be subject to careful monitoring and rigorous record keeping. A facility using restraint very frequently would be reevaluated by the regulatory body.

These are only some of the many features of the *Guidebook* which might be regarded as measures to prevent institutional abuse. More to the point, the *Guidebook* and the Consortium's efforts to implement the *Guidebook* are part of a comprehensive initiative to encourage and support high standards of residential care. The Consortium's humane and hopeful approach to the field will undoubtedly be shared by the vast majority of child care professionals. (For further information, contact the Consortium at the address given at the beginning of this article).

META-ABUSE: A PITFALL
FOR CHILD PROTECTION

ABUSING POOR CHILDREN
BY TRYING TO PROTECT THEM

Norman E. Silberberg
Margaret C. Silberberg

ABSTRACT. The authors argue that child protection attempts often actually harm children. Indicators of abuse, they point out, could also indicate poverty, and interventions that try to help children often actually harm them. Perhaps, the authors suggest, money spent to police abuse in families should be spread out so it can be used to assist families in need of relief *before* abuse occurs and to monitor those who say they are protecting children from their abusive parents.

Child abuse is not a recent phenomenon. Around 1890 American social work associations, federal agencies, clinics, and others all began to protect children from abuse. However, too frequently these agencies established to protect children from exploitation and harm became agents of the same exploitative and harmful treatment (Denzin, 1973). The juvenile court system, the schools, foster care, and the variety of other institutions that exist to reform or rehabilitate children often inadvertently brutalize and mistreat them while providing rather comfortable income for the adult helpers. Who watches these watchers?

The attempt of this paper is not to belittle honest attempts to protect

---

Requests for reprints should be addressed to Norman E. Silberberg and Margaret C. Silberberg, 920 Lincoln Ave., St. Paul, MN 55405.

133

children. Rather, it is to review the way this protection occurs. All too often, the system profits providers without assuring meaningful service to families. If these attempts at protecting children actually result in more breakup of families without benefits to the families' members, it is time to rethink the process to determine whether it is working. Too often pressures to prevent child abuse have only hung new regulations over the heads of the poor.

The American Humane Association developed a list of signals by which abuse or neglect can be detected. These signals include:

—being frequently absent from or late to school

—arriving at school too early or hanging around after class without reason

—being dressed in dirty or torn clothes, being unwashed, or being dressed inappropriately for the weather

—being shy and withdrawn

—needing, but not receiving, medical attention, such as dental work and eyeglasses

—sleeping in class

—having aggressive parents, parents who do not show up for appointments, or slovenly or dirty parents

—having parents whom the other parents or children do not know

There is little question as to who will be accused in this diagnostic game. It is much easier to be seen as a neglectful parent if you are poor than if you are rich.

Most writers agree that child abuse occurs in all socioeconomic classes but that most intervention occurs in the lower classes. Clearly, in poor homes proper medical care is a problem; there have been tomes written on the inability of the poor to gain access to the medical care system in any meaningful way or to pay for care if they enter the system. Tardiness may mean that a child is trying to avoid an inappropriate school program (which is the responsibility of the school, not the parent) or that older siblings have to help the child get ready for school while the parent is at work. Parents whose child is not successful in school may attempt to avoid the humiliation of returning to school to be told how bad the child is. According to this list, they must be accused of neglect for that. Even the child who dozes in class is suspect, though adults who doze through lectures are taken for granted.

The dangers in the descriptions cited above should be obvious to anyone concerned with civil liberties. Is the justified concern for a minority of children who are mistreated by their parents sufficient to allow teachers, public health nurses, school social workers, and others to make judgments about whether a family conforms to acceptable standards, especially when those standards most often represent the middle class majority? Is this not, in itself, abusive?

Are abused children better off when "helping agencies" intervene? Usually intervention is unequally applied, often it is ineffective, sometimes it is downright harmful. As Wald (1975) suggested in a critical review of intervention techniques, many cases of public intervention are unwarranted, and often the state takes too much control over child rearing.

Too often economic considerations dictate treatment. In one state, the school district must pay for most of a disturbed child's treatment unless the child is sent out of state. Thus, there is always a great deal of pressure to institutionalize children out of state. In addition, we have heard of psychiatrists and psychologists receiving kickbacks from institutions to which they refer clients. Who investigates these stories, and what is done if they are true? The emphasis on child abuse and neglect may create jobs for middle class people with little payoff to the potential recipients.

Sometimes the abuser benefits from the abuse. A 19-year-old woman reported on in a professional journal was unable to receive any support for raising her child, although she was poor. After she burned and lacerated her child, she received a college scholarship, day-care assistance, and other services. Had she not abused her child, she might still be living in poverty. Would it not be better if aid were provided before such serious calls for help arise?

Parents who harm their children are accused of child abuse, but if officials harm children, they can say they were rehabilitating the child. Jailing children is one such way of harming them. In 1975 an estimated 600,000 children were jailed pending their hearings. Many of them were not charged for crimes that would be crimes if committed by adults, but for status offenses because their lifestyles differed from the norm. Moreover, we have personally encountered the following types of abuse:

—a child shot and killed by a sheriff while accompanying another youngster driving a stolen car.

—a youngster in a juvenile facility handcuffed for hours at a time in a spread eagle position on a bare spring cot.

—children being removed from their "neglectful" Indian homes and placed in "good" Christian foster homes in areas so remote that the parents cannot visit the children, this lack of visitation then being viewed by the authorities as lack of interest! Some of these children may be placed in dozens of foster homes before they are 18. If foster homes are in short supply, we have seen brutal foster parents ignored by the watchers.

—behavior modification techniques including time-out rooms, electro-shock, slapping, and other techniques known in the scientific jargon as "negative"—in mental hospitals, clinics, and even schools.

—the wholesale drugging of children in order to achieve the narrow range of behavioral conformity that is tolerated in schools.

—youngsters being placed in psychiatric wards by their parents for such minor offenses as being caught smoking marijuana or attempting to live away from home before the age of legal majority. Almost invariably, the professionals in the mental health center cooperate by confining the youngsters and providing psychiatric "treatment." In addition, they provide mood-modifying substances which are legal, although the youths have been placed in there for using more benign, but illegal ones.

—members of the police tactical squad taking "troublemakers" into remote areas and "working them over."

—a youngster requiring stitches for being slammed up against the lockers by his teacher for not moving fast enough.

—police arbitrarily removing a family of children from their home in the evening while the parents are out and placing them in a shelter where the staff refuses to allow access to the parent.

Why did the child abuse fighters not prevent these events? Why are they concerned mostly about abuse done by parents?

Now that state intervention has been institutionalized, it is time to introduce some checks and balances to assure that overzealous pursuit of child abuse by schools and welfare departments does not result in more harm than good being done to the children. We would propose the establishment of community review teams, consisting of consumers and sympathetic service providers who would have investigative or appeal functions. Presently, parents accused of child abuse find the welfare system functioning as both judge and jury. The parents find themselves lined up alone against the county social worker, the county child abuse worker, the county attorney, the county psychologist, and the county judge. The parent participates in a process that may cost $20,000 or $30,000 a case but is unable to obtain the damage deposit for an apartment!

For some reason, our society is willing to spend large amounts for cure and little for prevention. We suggest that society examine the social forces and social institutions that lead to abuse and neglect rather than attempt to cure the situation on a case-by-case basis after it is too late. Perhaps the number of child abuse cases would be reduced if funds were allocated for the provision of money to the poor for whom children are a greater burden. Some of the resources could be allocated for 24-hour care centers where parents could drop children when the pressures of parenting become too difficult. Food and jobs could be provided. Homemaker services or periodic foster care could be made available to parents who cannot temporarily provide proper care to the family. The extended family could be paid to care for children.

In addition, enforcement should be equalized. Schools should not label children to assure conformity, to obtain parent cooperation, or to raise the statistics about neglect. If rules against child abuse and neglect are to be enforced, they should be enforced equally across socioeconomic levels.

Yet, as Wald (1975) said:

> Even handed application of the law should not mean depriving poor children of truly beneficial state intervention just because we are unwilling to identify middle-class children who also need help. The adoption of concrete standards . . . will not eliminate discretion, but it will limit interventions based solely on social worker's or judge's unsupported views about solid child rearing.

Heinous as actual child abuse is, it is time to review the system that attempts to control it to see that our resources are actually benefiting children.

REFERENCES

Denzin, N. *Children and their caretakers.* New Brunswick, NJ: Transaction Books, 1973.

Wald, M. State intervention on behalf of "neglected children": A search for realistic standards. *Stanford Law Review,* 1975, *27,* 985-1039.

PROTECTING ABUSED CHILDREN:
HELPING UNTIL IT HURTS

Bruce R. Thomas

ABSTRACT. The writer argues that the adoption of systematic methods of service delivery can lead to the failure of child welfare rather than to its success. He says that formulating rules for the response to abuse has caused the protective institutions to harm children because these rules break down informal helping systems.

I join together two concerns in this essay, words and children. Broadly, the subject is child abuse; more specifically, the subject is systemic and institutional abuse of children. The focus on words provides a means to analysis.

In the subtlety of words lies their power. To ignore that power is to increase the possibility of its abuse. We can learn much about the abuse of children by looking at the use and abuse of words in the revealing language of child welfare.

Language is revealing because it is a prime carrier of mythology. Our system of education largely confines the study of mythology to early chapters of human history; thus, we are blinded to the mythology in our present lives, where myths give meaning to personal action and social events, for myths, as Murray Edelman reminds us in *Political Language*, need not be fiction. Myths answer an enduring human need.

The need that myth fulfills becomes larger as the gap between what was as citizens want to do and what we actually can do widens because of society's social and economic arrangements. The gap must be explained, and myth provides such explanations—with language its readiest medium.

To inquire into the language—and therefore the mythology—of child abuse in its systemic and institutional forms, I use a simple method. When certain words recur in the vocabulary of child welfare services, I ask

Bruce R. Thomas is affiliated with Chicago Associates for Social Research, 410 S. Michigan Ave., Chicago, IL 60605. Requests for reprints should be addressed to Bruce Thomas at that address.

several questions. Why are certain words chosen? What are the consequences of choosing those words rather than other words? To whom are
the chosen words directed?

Such questioning of words is rarely practiced—and for good reason. A
close examination of the language of child welfare shows that failure is
often covered up and success is limited. Moreover, the covering and the
limiting are bonded. If we wish to undo the limitation and more successfully address the problems signaled by child abuse, we need to unmask the
failure.

My conclusion is that the source of failure in child welfare is precisely
that which is often held to be the source of its actual or potential success:
the adoption of systemic methods of service delivery. In the pages that
follow, as I trace out the route to this unsettling conclusion, I will com-
mute regularly between the concrete and the abstract. I will begin with the
concrete.

Two Portraits of Child Abuse

Jonathan

Jonathan is 4 years old. His hair is a wind-blown spinnaker of black
curls, his khaki-hued body a lithe and powerful hull. This mission of this
swift-running sloop is exploration and discovery.

Jonathan's mother is Leonine: 22 years old, herself lithe and lively.
What she shares with Jonathan is what divides them; for Leonine, in
making it possible for Jonathan to explore and discover, forecloses her
own exploration. She wishes to return to school and then to work. But she
cannot; the management of Jonathan is a daily, relentless responsibility.
The father, Boyd, is set largely to the task of provisioning his household;
he works at two jobs and has only part of Sunday at home. Leonine and
Jonathan are cast together each day, all day, throughout the week.

The tension erupts one day in early spring. Jonathan has been in full
exercise on his mission, running, looking, asking questions. In a burst of
motion, he tips over a table; a glass and two dishes break. Leonine ex-
plodes; she slaps Jonathan and throws him against a wall. Instantly con-
trite but her anger not yet spent, she seizes a heavy ashtray and flings it
across the room. It strikes a cupboard, smashes glass, and tumbles noisily
to the floor. Jonathan, bleeding from the nose and bruised on the shoul-
der, flees out the door of the apartment, down the stairs, and out into the
street.

On the street, fear and bewilderment fuse with terror. He runs. A policeman, Will, sees the flight and blood. He stops his car, catches Jonathan, holds him in his arms. Words gasped out between sobs sketch the event. The scenario is familiar to Will, and his duty clear: he is to make a report. Yet instead he returns to his car with Jonathan in his arms and asks his partner to drive down the street to Delma's. Delma runs a small neighborhood grocery store; Will knows her. Jonathan still in his arms, he enters the store and asks Delma if she knows Jonathan. She does. Jonathan is transferred from one set of arms to another. Deft fingers dab away blood from his nose. The bruise is inspected. A lollipop is brought into view, regarded, then taken. Jonathan is transferred back to Will's arms; Delma disappears through a back door. She calls Leonine, tells her that she has Jonathan and that he is not seriously hurt. Will tends the store while Delma goes to see Leonine. Within the hour, Jonathan is home.

When Will asks Delma later who might help in the problem, Delma thinks of her pastor's wife, Florida. She calls Florida that evening and describes the event and the family. Delma talks to Leonine over the next grocery transaction, focusing not on Jonathan but on Leonine and how she is feeling, and mentioning Florida. Leonine says she will think about talking to Florida.

A few days later, she agrees, and Florida makes a visit. In the talks that follow, Florida retrieves and shares her memories of the tensions and conflicts of motherhood. The sharing begins to dissolve the shame in Leonine's mind; her feelings for Jonathan become a bond with Florida instead of a prison for herself. She is able to say that Jonathan is both her joy and her despair. Florida sketches the possibilities: immediately, an informal child-care group made up of mothers in the church; later, with Jonathan's enrollment in school, a return to college on state scholarship funds.

Leonine's future possibilities lend her calm for the present. The problem is not solved; problems rarely are, in any final sense. But she can hope, and from the harbor of that hope, the good sloop Jonathan sails again on its ancient, happy mission.

Robert

Robert is a 10 year old among the 8 and 9 year olds in Mrs. Jackson's third-grade class. A soft, round face topped by disheveled thick blond hair contrasts sharply with the leanness of his body; his skin stretches taut on the bone frame. He is quick in dodge ball, but quick also to tire. He is silent in class, never offers words, often declines the invitation to speak. His eyes are all feral alertness. His occasional speech hints at Appalachia.

The third time that Robert comes to class without a warm jacket, Mrs. Jackson decides to act. She speaks to Mr. Slater, the school social worker. Robert Cottle, she says, does not seem to have any winter clothes; he sometimes comes to school without socks; he needs dental care. Mr. Slater agrees to talk with Robert.

The man and boy meet at the end of a school day. Robert is evasive and noncommital. Mr. Slater is able only to elicit minimal details; a home with both parents present, three other children, all younger than Robert. Mr. Slater asks Mrs. Jackson to keep him posted.

Robert appears again without a jacket—and limping. Asked about the limp, he alludes vaguely to an accident. The passage of a week brings more jacketless days. Apprised, Mr. Slater decides to act; he calls the state welfare agency to report the possibility of abuse and neglect.

The agency sends a child abuse worker to Robert's home. Miss Gaines finds that the home is a third-floor walk-up apartment in a neighborhood of littered streets and abandoned cars. The line of buildings on the Cottle's street is broken by empty lots whose detritus evokes images of buildings abandoned, vandalized, torched, and destroyed.

Mrs. Cottle's apartment, however, defies the ambience of the street. It is neat, sparsely furnished but meticulously clean. Mrs. Cottle is home with the youngest child, a 2-year-old girl. Miss Gaines explains that she works for the child welfare agency and that the agency has learned of the school's concern about Robert's clothes. She chooses her words carefully; she must veil the possible accusation.

Mrs. Cottle will have none of it. "Why are you here?" she asks. The blunt question, enforced by directness of eye, absolved Miss Gaines of the need for euphemism and indirection. But she will still honor Mrs. Cottle's dignity by couching her role in words that are softly abstract; she terms herself a social worker rather than a child abuse worker and repeated her opening remark: "The school suggested that Robert needs some warm clothes and we might be able to help."

"We have no money for Robert's clothes," Mrs. Cottle says. Her dress, its print long faded from the cotton, substantiates her response. Miss Gaines reaches down to her handbag on the floor and extracts a large brown thermos. "I have some hot tea," she says. "I couldn't get through the day without it. Would you like some?" she asks. Mrs. Cottle produces two cups, and they talk over tea for an hour.

Back at her office, Miss Gaines writes her report. Her own summary is given to a friend that night, over dinner:

> "The Cottle family is just poor. They don't have any money. They came here from Kentucky a few months ago. The father thought he could find a job immediately through a relative who works in a factory here. But there wasn't any job. They had money when they arrived, but it's gone. The father's been able to get some part-time work, but not enough to support the family. He won't go on welfare; he seems to be a very proud man. Mrs. Cottle loves her husband; her pride is his pride. I get the sense that the father is getting a little desperate. I finally asked Mrs. Cottle about Robert's limp. She told me that his father hit him in a moment of frustrated rage. The father's quite strict. But I think Robert loves him and respects him—and probably has a good bit of his pride, too. The father just needs to find a job.

He finds no job, although he pursues every avenue possible, including some suggested by Miss Gaines. Full winter comes. Robert stops coming to school. Reports are made. Miss Gaines comes again to the Cottle apartment. She finds Mrs. Cottle and two of her children in the kitchen, huddled around a small electric heater, two cans of pork and beans on the table.

Miss Gaines finds an emergency shelter for the Cottles, where they can stay for a month. The measure of security and warmth seems to help Mr. Cottle; he finds a job in a warehouse. But on the eighth day of work, he injures his leg. The injury precludes work for an indefinite period.

Miss Gaines remains confident that the family can hold together and weather the setbacks. She offers to put the four children in emergency foster care for a month or so, while the father recovers and the mother looks for work. The Cottles agree reluctantly. Mrs. Cottle finds a job as a department store clerk and, shortly after, locates a small apartment for herself and Mr. Cottle in a hotel.

Robert, however, will not accept the foster care situation. He cannot understand the separation from his parents. At every opportunity, he runs to see them. En route one night, he is picked up by the police; he refuses to give his name and address. A report to the child welfare agency finally establishes his identity. He is returned to the foster home, but the foster parents find Robert unmanageable. Emergency foster care has been extended a month, but the foster parents will not keep Robert any longer and call Miss Gaines.

Miss Gaines is no longer the caseworker assigned to the Cottles. After agency reorganization, Mr. Gray is the caseworker. He has glanced through the Cottle file; the phone call from the foster parents sends him back to it for a more careful reading. A year out of social work school, Mr. Gray is deeply committed to permanency planning. Since the parents still cannot provide for the children, emergency foster care will be continued for the three younger Cottles, but not for Robert, who is clearly troubled, his uncommunicativeness almost autistic. Other arrangements will be made.

Some months later, Miss Gaines calls Mr. Gray to inquire about the Cottles. Mr. Gray is pleased; Mr. Cottle has recovered from his injury and found steady work. They have a new apartment, large enough for the children; the three children are at home again with their parents. "And Robert?" Miss Gaines asks. "Robert is still in the institution," says Mr. Gray.

"What institution?" asks Miss Gaines, stunned. Mr. Gray tells her. "Why?" asks Miss Gaines. Mr. Gray tells her that Robert is emotionally disturbed, that the foster parents found him unmanageable, and that the institutional prognosis is guarded. Robert may need protracted care before he can return home. "He has been violent," says Mr. Gray, "and uncooperative and resistant to treatment." Miss Gaines says to Mr. Gray, "Oh God," and to herself, "That didn't have to happen."

In helping Jonathan, Will never reported Leonine's moment of violence; in official terms, therefore, the incident never occurred. Nevertheless, it did occur, and four of its aspects stand out.

The first is the physical quality of the attention to Jonathan. From the moment Will picked him up until the time he was returned home, Jonathan was held. He was a terrified child and needed, above all, comfort and reassurance. What better comfort and reassurance than the cradle of adult arms?

Second, the attention of Will and Delma shifted to Leonine once Jonathan was comforted. Jonathan was interpreted, quickly, accurately, wordlessly, as a message from Leonine.

Third, the response to Leonine was informal and voluntary. No one was required to do anything, yet Delma accepted the obligation to help by talking to Florida. Florida accepted the obligation to help and offered to talk to Leonine. Leonine had to choose herself to talk with Florida.

Fourth, Will was effective because he was insubordinate. He did what he was not supposed to do, for in substituting his own judgment for the dictates of law and procedure, he violated the law.

The portrait of Robert constrasts sharply with that of Jonathan, where the signature of bureaucracy was large. Official actors were involved, reports and referrals made, procedures set in motion, official resources used.

Yet Will and Miss Gaines were more similar than different. Each knew how to wear the official uniform lightly. Both had learned to cultivate personal discretion in the midst of official bureaucracy.

The difference between the two was that officialdom finally overtook Miss Gaines. She was compelled to use an official resource because that was the only way she could address the Cottles' need. Emergency foster care was an indirect form of financial assistance.

For Robert the consequences of official resources unfolded to a senseless outcome. The change in setting, however benign and temporary, profoundly unsettled him. In the temporary foster care setting, his actions were interpreted differently than they had been at home. That set a process in motion that ended with the institutionalization of Robert. Indeed, he was *made* into a child welfare case. Yet the transformation was no one's intent. How then did it happen?

It happened because of the limits within which Miss Gaines had to work, limits that affected not only what she could do but when she could do it. For the Cottles, the need was money, but not only money, for money, to be effective, has to be married to the moment and to its source.

The Cottles needed money immediately; timing was therefore crucial. Yet their acceptance of money depended also on the creation of a measure of trust between Miss Gaines and Mrs. Cottle. The Cottles were fiercely independent and distrustful of welfare. Miss Gaines understood them and knew that she had to establish a personal relationship with Mrs. Cottle. The emblem of her sensitivity was the thermos filled with hot tea; produced out of the volume of her handbag, it could evoke a warmth beyond itself, such that Miss Gaines and Mrs. Cottle became Fran Gaines and Eleanor Cottle having a cup of tea together. Within that context, money from Miss Gaines would have become as expression of human obligation which implies reciprocity; the Cottles would have found a way of reciprocating.

Miss Gaines, however, could not provide money at all; she was therefore precluded from the exercise of her skills. She could only approximate a response to the need for money. The result for Robert was an incarceration that came to justify itself over time. The result for the Cottles was loss.

Over time, through a transformation by modern social recordkeeping, that loss was made into an official success because permanency planning had been achieved; three of the Cottle children were returned home after a period of emergency foster care. Robert was under care in an institution and would be returned home eventually. Statistics will not reveal that the Robert separated from his parents will not be the Robert returned to them.

The portraits of Jonathan and Robert reveal the human detail of success through noncompliance and failure caused by the system and masked by it. Perhaps the truly systematic outcomes of a child welfare system are malign rather than benign. We can test the possibility by asking two questions: What is the assignment given to the child protection system? How is that system set up to fulfill its assignment?

The Assignment of the Child Welfare System

A careful look at the term *child abuse* will reveal much about the assignment, because it is the label now used to justify thousands of official interventions into private lives. The term initially seems clear; we understand *child* and *abuse*. The two together evoke clear images of specific adult actions (or non-actions) that injure children.

Yet if we treat incidents of child abuse as messages that require interpretation, clarity soon recedes. The interpretive trail leads back to adults. Will and Miss Gaines both interpreted the children as signals from their parents that help was needed. The needs of the children were in both instances easily and readily met. The real needs were those of adults.

The term child abuse is therefore an oblique way of talking about adult needs and troubles. The child is a messenger. The sum of all the messages sent to a child welfare agency in the course of a year amounts to a catalog of our national social problems and pressures, including poverty, poor education, alcoholism and drug abuse, crime, urban slums, inflation, deterioration of communal life, competitiveness, and doubtless others as well. Perhaps the most that can be said is that child abuse is a moment of revelation in which adults unveil their responses to a set of social forces with which they must cope. Every act of child abuse is individual personality interacting with larger societal circumstances.

We might then say that the assignment of the child welfare system is to alter individual adult behavior or circumstances—while remaining utterly powerless to alter the broader social settings to which individual behavior or circumstance is intimately connected.

How is a child welfare agency set up to meet this assignment? A close look at four aspects of the child welfare system will suggest some answers. These four aspects are its organization, its resources, its relationship to the private sector, and its legal environment.

Organization

Child welfare agencies are often governmental bureaucracies, organized either on a county or statewide basis. Their form is the traditional pyramid: at the top, the director; one level down, deputy directors; at the third level, subadministrators. Further division of responsibility and authority continues on down through the widening levels of the pyramid.

Only at the bottom of the pyramid does the responsibility held by one person broaden out again. Indeed, each caseworker on the front line, working with the men and women who need help, is in effect a mini-director, confronted and affected by all aspects of the agency's functioning. The director is best understood, then, as a symbol of the caseworker at the front line—for it is these two whose work and scope of responsibility are most identical.

Yet the two live in utterly different and separate universes, each universe with its own discipline. The discipline of the front line is shaped by the need to respond to men and women who signal the need for help through their children. The discipline of the director's office is shaped by the need to respond to legislatures and elected officials of the executive branch, to organize child welfare interests, to the state government in some cases, to the federal government in all cases—and to the needs and issues generated by the bureaucracy itself.

The consequences of these different disciplines are multiple and malign. Upward mobility within the pyramid requires that the caseworker abandon the discipline of the front line and adopt the discipline of the pyramid's top. This switch in allegiance means that competence at the front line—where it is most needed—is a dead-end. One cannot remain at the front line and enjoy the increases in salary and status that most people expect in a career. The pyramid, therefore, systematically either draws people up and away from the front line or else forces them out altogether.

Moreover, the competence required for upward mobility within the pyramid is generally antithetical to competence at the front line. Upward mobility requires attentiveness of the imperatives contrived within the organizational pyramid and shaped at the pyramid's top. Upward striving becomes an increasingly isolated drive, for the competition becomes narrower as opportunities narrow toward the top of the pyramid. Trust is replaced by caution. Language becomes more cautious, and the inclination to use rote language more pronounced.

The contrast between the ethics and atmosphere of upward striving within the pyramid and the ethics and atmosphere of casework at the front lines is stark. To begin with, the real authority of a gifted supervisor at the front lines is not that conferred by the pyramid, but that earned by competence, experience, and sensitivity. Further, effectiveness at the front lines involves teamwork, whether formal or informal. A team of caseworkers is invariably more than the sum of its individual human parts; it involves a curious alchemy, wherein the team expresses a collective strength that overcomes individual weaknesses. By collaboration, the sharing of knowledge and resources, the development of trust and informal communication, the team evolves a character that works to the benefit of men and women in need of help.

Such an entity is fragile to the touch of the more rigid, authoritarian pyramid. And with depressing frequency, the pyramid does systematically rupture the growth of a team by reorganizations, by driving off both workers and supervisors, by lifting front line competence away into the upper reaches of the pyramid.

The harms of the pyramid organization are not noticed, because they are so familiar. Their impact on the front line is felt daily and is the stuff of much conversation among front line workers, but familiarity leads to resignation, and the pyramid seems inevitable.

As if the systematically malignant consequences of the pyramidal form on effective casework were not enough, another aspect of systematic organization adds more difficulties. A child welfare agency forms one part of the larger social response system. The larger system is neatly divided into clearly defined fiefdoms. Public aid handles cash assistance and medical costs; mental health handles the mentally disturbed; vocational rehabilitation handles the problems of drug and alcohol abuse. Each fiefdom abides by its own definition of eligibility, controls its own set of resources.

The result was clear on Robert. Miss Gaines could not obtain money for the Cottles because the division and subdivision of resources in the social response system lock its front line workers into tightly defined roles that constrict their effectiveness.

Resources

The word *resource* recurs in the vocabulary of child welfare. It normally refers to such items as foster homes, group homes, counseling and psychiatric services, emergency shelters, and the like. The issue raised by the word is vital: A caseworker must have resources to be effective. But what are we talking about when we use the word *resource*?

Clearly, caseworkers' first resources are themselves. Miss Gaines, a resourceful, perceptive, wily yet sensitive person, illuminates just how powerful this resource can be. Day in, day out, she can count on one instrument, herself.

The fact that her own organization defeats her is no accident. Unable to provide money to the Cottles, she is therefore unable to work the kind of magic that good caseworkers can sometimes perform. That magic is a blending of human skills with material resources, such that assistance can be rendered wtih obligation and trust.

A second and fundamental resource is the organization itself. Were it arranged to acknowledge the primacy of the front line role, it would buttress and support the front line worker at every point. But it is not so arranged, and because it is not so arranged, staff training becomes a feckless effort, inevitably frustrated by an organizational setting fundamentally antithetical to the development of human resources.

A third resource is the group of services and settings that is usually denoted by the term *resource*: foster homes, group homes, and the like. Yet far more often than we might care to believe, the resource uses the client rather than the reverse. Miss Gaines, in using emergency foster care, forced the Cottles to adapt to the agency. Sometimes such adaptation is harmless; in Robert's case, it was not.

The harm done to Robert was compounded by an injury to the state treasury. As a consequence of the inability to provide a small amount of cash assistance, the state incurred a total expenditure of $30,000 to cover 2 years of institutionalization for Robert.

Since resources of the third category are often purchased by a child welfare agency from the private sector, they will be examined in the section to follow.

Public-Private Relationship

Over a period of decades, welfare has changed from a private, philan-
thropic character to a public, tax-supported character. Government is
now the dominant force; its influence is stronger than its dollars might
suggest because its policies strongly influence the use of private dollars.
The distinction between public and private has become, in fact, increasingly blurred.

Yet, however indistinct in practice the line is between public and private, it nonetheless lives on through the contractual relationship between
public and private agencies: the public agency purchases services from the
private agencies.

The effect of this policy is largely ignored. The purchase of care creates
a market in social services. The currency of this market includes not only
children, but also the old poor, the indigent sick, and others. Government
policy fashions out of such people a new identity; they become warrants
on the state purse.

In other words, they are monetized. An old poor person represents so
much money each month to a nursing home. A child needing a foster
home represents a sum of money that government will pay each month.
The conversion of the warrant into cash is, of course, a process invisible
to the monetized human being; forms are filled out, invoices prepared,
and checks eventually sent directly to the provider from the state treasury.

To monetize human beings is to create the possibility of exploitation.
The possibility becomes clear by looking at a hypothetical private agency
that contracts with a state agency to provide, say, foster care for 500
children. The private agency commits itself to the provision of such care;
it must find foster parents, hire foster care workers, provide offices for the
workers. To make income match expenditure, 500 children must be referred to the agency—for it is only the arrival of a child that triggers
money from the state agency and only the continued presence of a child in
the private foster care system that assures the steady flow of money.

Such an arrangement creates a condition conducive to systemic incarceration: children become trapped in a system that moves them from one
foster home to another. The longer they remain in the system, the less
likely is their return to their biological parents, the more they are damaged, and the more difficult they are to adopt.

In short, the private agency as a market institution has a fixed investment in plant and labor, the cost of which must be met by an income flow
that the private agency cannot fully control. The flow is determined by the

state. The private agency therefore can only control the children whom it has in care. So the basic, underlying incentive for the agency is to keep those children in care, rather than aggressively pushing children out of the system and into biological or adoptive homes.

The stark and impersonal language of the market fits uneasily and awkwardly into the benign and altruistic language of child welfare. However, the blunt fact is that a market has been created and a market mentality is therefore required. The economic facts cannot be wished away.

The actual impact of the market mentality on children varies, of course. In some private agencies, children are effectively protected from the rawness of the economic calculus; the leadership of such agencies is vested in men and women who refuse to be warped by the forces unleashed upon them by a market and who do their best to do well by the children.

The fact remains, however, that the larger system involved in the public-private contractual relationship creates the possibilities for systematic abuse of children. The realization of such possibilities is not theoretical; the work of groups like the Children's Defense Fund has provided ample documentation of the realities of systematic abuse.

The Legal Environment of Child Welfare

Child welfare is made possible by a statutorily sanctioned extension of state power into the privacy of the family. When adult impotence or incompetence expresses itself in the abuse or neglect of children, the state provides itself with the grounds for intervention in order to exercise control over the children and, sometimes, to levy punishment on the adults.

The child welfare agency therefore has dual and contradictory roles: those of helper and prosecutor. The contradiction is fundamental. It is virtually impossible to be an adroit interpreter and an adept investigator at the same time. The contradiction is recognized in some child welfare agencies by splitting the roles. Yet that only represents an adjustment to the contradiction; it does not remove it.

As child abuse has steadily become more important as a rubric under which children are drawn into child welfare systems, a wider and wider net has been set for its detection, investigation, and prevention. More and more people are now required under the law to make official reports if such abuse is suspected. In effect, individual states have created networks of informers. The goal of such networks is of course benign; the goal is fashioned out of some notion of the best interests of the children. But what are the consequences?

One consequence is that a child welfare agency contributes to the corrosion of the very resource upon which it depends heavily: the informal community. The response to Jonathan by Will, Delma, and Florida is an example of the informal community at work. If the informal community responses to child abuse did not exist, child welfare agencies would be even more swamped with child abuse than they are presently. A doctor or teacher or public health nurse who knows a family within the context of community life has every reason in the world to avoid invocation of the state authority and procedures and to use informal means of response. The higher one goes in the socioeconomic scale, the more likely the informal response becomes.

In many situations, where no community, much less an informal community, exists, there is no alternative for formal state intervention. Yet this fact should not justify an evolving social policy that makes informal responses to child abuse illegal. Such a policy works to exacerbate those stresses and pressures that are already working to sap the strengths and durability of community and neighborhood life in the United States.

This diffusion of the legal net woven by child abuse also works to obscure an extraordinary omission in the law: the accountability of the state for its abuse and neglect of children. The child welfare system is effectively immune from prosecution. When the state removes children from their homes and incarcerates them in a system that moves them serially from one foster home to another, the state is clearly abusing the children. But who is accountable?

It is by no means clear that the legal environment surrounding child abuse is a positive force in the prevention and response to child abuse; and it is certainly possible that it compounds the problems.

Each of these four aspects of the child welfare system contributes its own particular sets of obstacles, frustrations, and constraints. The four together interact in a myriad of ways to create yet more obstacles, frustrations, and constraints. The net result is that the child welfare system can only work in spite of itself.

That it does work in spite of itself is clear. Particular families and their children are sometimes assisted expeditiously and skillfully; other families are more slowly, painfully knitted back together again; and yet other families are accepted as casualties, but their children are placed in alternative settings that provide genuine and consistent affection and care.

Such achievement is not systemic. It is personal: the achievement is an artifact, the product of individual human action and interaction. The real world of casework in the realm of child abuse is not evoked by the standard vocabulary of bureaucratic job descriptions, but by an alternative vocabulary that would include such words as diplomacy, magic, justice, and obligation.

Diplomacy. Effective caseworkers are perforce adroit diplomats. They are constantly negotiating, within their agencies and without, with other service agencies, with courts, with relatives.

Magic. Caseworkers, to be effective, must be alchemists, must work alterations in the very quality and character of things, such that they become invested in human meaning. The laboratory of alchemy is the invisible realm of understanding that can be created by two human beings. It is an intangible, recognized by its absence.

Justice. Caseworkers are agents of justice in an injust world. In moments of crisis in the lives of other human beings, they are responsible for decisions, for the selection of information that will affect the decisions of others, for the invocation of public resources, all of which can profoundly affect the quality and direction of these other human lives.

Obligation. In a world deprived a little more each day of the informal ties of obligation, caseworkers must somehow themselves express and further create webs of obligation in the lives of children. A child's supreme entitlement is to live in a web of obligation, peopled by men and women who have chosen to accept obligation. When the web is fragile or ripped, the caseworker must either seek to repair it or to find an alternative web. Neither is easy; both require all the diplomacy and magic that caseworkers can muster.

The world evoked by words like *diplomat, magician,* and *judge* contrasts strangely and sharply with the world evoked by the emerging official language of child welfare. This new official language is the language of systems. Its central notion is the idea of a "social service delivery system." Computers figure pervasively. Directors of child welfare agencies speak bravely to legislators of their progress in the installation of service configurations that deliver high quality services calibrated to produce maximum benefits at minimal cost.

The official language is clearly mythical. Its purpose is that of reassurance. It reassures both speaker and audience that progress is being made, that problems are being solved. Its consequence is deception. The language masks the failure of the system to meet its assignment—and also conceals the ways in which nonsystematic methods actually work.

The official language has little meaning for caseworkers; but it is not intended for caseworkers. It is intended for legislators, government bureaucrats, foundations, and all other officials of institutions involved in the funding and administration of child welfare agencies.

That the official language is mythical is not so much a criticism as an explanation that illuminates its real purposes and its real audience. Its ultimate purpose—one that lies behind the purpose of reassurance and the consequence of deception—is to obscure the emergence of the child welfare into a place within the American political economy.

Child welfare and its kindred agencies in the larger welfare network now occupy an established place in the American political economy. Government has created a market for social services. The creation of a market means that supply has come forth to meet demand. It also means that supply now requires the demand.

To say that supply now requires a demand is to say that welfare agencies are as dependent upon their clients as the clients are upon the welfare agencies. Agencies of the welfare system have become institutionalized, which requires in turn the institutionalization of the problems they address.

This does not mean that the individuals who run such agencies either wish or in any direct way promote the continuation of the problems they are supposed to solve. It means that the underlying structure of the world they inhabit effectively precludes them from doing anything other than servicing (as opposed to solving) the problems they are to confront.

Because welfare administrators cannot be explicit about their real role, they are forced to adopt a language that obscures the relationship between problem and problem solver and that expresses in some measure the deeply held American belief in progress and our ability to solve social problems. The systems language serves this need nicely.

The government-created market in social services has several forms of currency. Children are one; the old poor, the indigent sick, and the indigent disturbed are others. Governmental policy has monetized such people. Human beings who are monetized are made part of a market setting are potentially subject to abuse and exploitation. That this potential is realized has been documented again and again. That it will be realized more often is inevitable when economic circumstances force the actors in the welfare market to pay heed ever more carefully and consistently to the economic calculus.

INDEX

Abusers, characteristics of 16-18, 61,
116-125
Causes of abuse
inherent in child care work 16-18, 19,
21, 115-124, 128-129
inherent in psychiatric care 83-84,
85-86
arising from unreachable children 99-
107
arising from responses to abuse 133-
137, 139-159
Child abuse and neglect
in families 3, 7, 15-22, 23-45, 139-146
cause for institutionalization 7-8, 89-92
compared to institutional abuse 25-33
characteristics of victims of 15-16, 81-
82
characteristics of abusers 16-18
See also Institutional abuse, Corporal
punishment
Child care workers
conditions of, leading to use of force
16-18, 19-21, 83-84, 85-86, 115-
125, 128-129, 146-154
training of 41, 80-81, 128
Child protection services
role of 24-25, 33-40, 111-112, 146-154
Child welfare system
See Child protection services
Children's Defense Fund 151
Children's rights
to development 3, 24, 25, 33
to health care 76-77
in psychiatric care 82-85, 89-98
limitations of 106-107
Control
as intervention 26, 30-33
in schools 47-55
in hospitals 82-85
policies about 130-132
Corporal punishment 4

definition of 49
in schools 47-55
religious defense of 57-63
Court involvement
in residential placement 89-98
in corporal punishment 52-55

Educateur model 18-19

Foster care drift 11-12

Guidebook on Residential Child Care 129-
132

Health needs
of institutionalized juveniles 65-77

Interstate Consortium of Residential
Child Care 129-132
Institutional abuse
definition of 3-4, 9, 24, 33-40
types of 9-12
extent of 8-9
victims of, characteristics 15-16, 81-82,
103-105
abusers, characteristics of 16-18, 61,
115-125
compared to family abuse 15-22, 34-
36, 80-86
causes of 16-18, 19, 21, 83-84, 85-86,
99-107, 115-124, 128-129, 133-137,
139-154
policies pertaining to 8, 13, 23-45, 47-
48, 54-55, 58-59, 89-98, 116, 121-
123, 129-132, 151-154
responsibility for 27-29, 33-40
reporting of 8-9, 24, 39-40, 40-42
prevention of 4, 36-40, 94-96, 121-123,
127-132
responses to 4, 109-110
investigation of 42-45